RISE ABOVE ADVERSITY

HOW TO OVERCOME AND STEER THROUGH DIFFICULT TIMES

BRIAN TRACY AND

OTHER LEADING ENTREPRENEURS AND PROFESSIONALS

Foreword by:
Shishir Lakhani, BSc, PQS, DTM
Heart and Stroke Foundation - Past Member of the Board of
Directors, Associated Senior Executives - Vice President

NORTHSTAR SUCCESS

RISE ABOVE ADVERSITY: HOW TO OVERCOME AND STEER THROUGH DIFFICULT TIMES

This is a work of non-fiction. Any resemblance of names, personal characteristics, and details of people, living or dead, is coincidental and unintentional. The reader is solely responsible for their actions and results. The authors are responsible for their content and their opinions. If professional or legal advice is required, readers should seek the service of a competent professional.

For bulk orders for promotions, fundraising and educational use, please contact North Star Success for special discounts. Book excerpts can be created as needed.

Published by North Star Success Inc.

🌐 www.northstarsuccess.com
✉ support@northstarsuccess.com
📞 +1 647 479 0790

FOREWORD

We have and are still enduring the worldwide COVID pandemic.

It has in many instances tested us, challenged us and unfortunately lacerated so many of us.

Such times certainly test our resilience and our grit. Upon survival we may enjoy post traumatic growth. They say adversity helps to strengthen us and builds our character.

Rise above Adversity brings a message of hope and shows us the intrinsic human ability to manage distress even in the midst of dire times.

It is indeed a bonus that North Star Success has selected several contributing authors to share their relatable difficult experiences; *Rise above Adversity* provides multiple options, solutions and strategies.

This book provides to one and all, in any field, inspirational new interpretations of issues and their subsequent creative solutions.

Life provides its ups and its downs. The authors show us how each of them personally managed and steered through what seemed like unsurmountable challenges.

Like many in business, I, too, have seen and lived through many turbulent times. I, as a founder and an entrepreneur, can certainly relate to the authors in this book.

Not unlike many, I have experienced the roller coaster that we call life. I have seen the booms and the busts of the economic cycles.

In my case, it took passionate teamwork. We were even able to convert our adversities into opportunities. I am grateful to all, directly and indirectly who made my success possible. I consider myself fortunate to have been able to successfully retire at an early age.

Having founded my manufacturing business serving the construction industry, I am well versed in juggling many hats. I went through my twenty-seven-year learning curve. I am proud to say I still continue to learn and improve.

Being part of the cyclical construction sector, it was always a challenge to correctly time growth to synchronize with the building cycle.

The recessions were deep and bruising; they separated the 'boys from the men,' as they say.

Being well planned and resourced gave us a chance to weather the storm, stay alive and reap the benefits, once the recovery phase kicked in.

Being actively retired, I still continue to give back to the health sector and the business community.

A profound lesson learnt; there is no wealth if there is no health.

So I have spent many fruitful years and dedicated much effort with Heart and Stroke Foundation (where I served as a member of the Board of Directors).

I also continue to volunteer at Associated Senior Executives where we (retired Entrepreneurs and Executives act as a Board of Advisors) offer timely business guidance.

This much I do know, passing on a lifelong learning to others makes me for one, a much more fulfilled and a better student of life.

I have known Dr. Shahab Anari for many years, and I can say without any hesitation that he is the ideal person to bring such a book of resilience to life.

I congratulate Shahab for utilizing his connections and tapping into personal stories from so many (often from the world of business) to make this book *Rise above Adversity* a very relevant read, especially in the present times.

Shishir Lakhani, BSc, PQS, DTM
Heart and Stroke Foundation - Past Member of the Board
of Directors, Associated Senior Executives - Vice President

Contents:

Developing
Resilience
in Difficult Times

Brian Tracy

Developing Resilience in Difficult Times

Brian Tracy

Your life will be a series of ups and downs, successes and failures, no matter what you do to guard against them. Peter Drucker, the management guru, said that the one thing that is inevitable in the life of the leader is the *crisis*. The only thing that matters is how you respond to the unavoidable crises that you will have on a regular basis.

The great historian, Arnold Toynbee, after studying the twenty-six great civilizations of history, found that each of them started small and grew based on their ability to respond effectively to the unexpected challenges they faced over time. He called this the "crisis-response theory of history." It was their ability to accept responsibility, without blaming or complaining, that determined their long-term success or failure. My favorite affirmation, no matter what happens, are the words, "I am responsible," repeated over and over until you feel in complete control of the situation.

Practice No Limit Thinking

You have the ability, right now, to earn vastly more than you are earning today, probably two or three times as much, just to start off. How do we know this? Simple. You are surrounded by people who are not as smart, as ambitious or as determined as you - who are already earning much more than you are. And all of these people started off earning less than you are earning today. In this chapter, I will show you how to move to the front of the income line of life, and faster than you ever thought possible. You will learn how to influence others in every area of your financial life.

One of the qualities of superior men and women is that they are extremely *self-reliant*. They accept complete responsibility for themselves and everything that happens to them. They look to themselves as the source of their successes and as the main cause of their problems and difficulties. High achievers say, "If it's to be, it's up to me."

When things aren't moving along as fast as they want, they ask themselves, "What is it *in me* that is causing this problem?" They refuse to make excuses or to blame other people. Instead, they look into themselves, and seek for ways to overcome their obstacles and to make progress.

See Yourself as Self Employed

Totally self-responsible people look upon themselves as *self-employed*. They see themselves as the presidents of their own personal services corporations. They realize that no matter who signs their paycheck, in the final analysis they work for themselves. Because they have this attitude of self-employment, they take a strategic approach to their work and to their lives.

The essential element in strategic planning for a corporation or a business entity is the concept of *"return on equity (ROE)."* All business planning is aimed at organizing and reorganizing the activities and resources of the business in such a way as to increase the *financial* returns to the business owners. It is to increase the quantity of output relative to the quantity of input. It is to focus on areas of high potential profitability and return and, simultaneously, to withdraw resources from areas of lower profitability and return. Companies that do this effectively in a rapidly changing environment are the ones that survive and prosper. Companies that fail to do this form of strategic analysis are those that fall behind and often disappear.

To achieve everything you are capable of achieving as a person, you also must become a skilled strategic planner with regard to your life and work. But instead of aiming to increase your return on equity, your goal is to increase your return on *energy.*

Most people in America, and worldwide, start off with little more than their ability to work. More than 80 percent of the millionaires in America started with nothing. Most successful people have been broke, or nearly broke, several times during their younger years. But the ones who eventually get to the top are those who do certain things in certain ways, and those actions set them apart from the masses.

Perhaps the most important thing they do, consciously or unconsciously, is to look at themselves strategically, thinking about how they can better use themselves in the marketplace;

how they can best capitalize on their strengths and abilities to increase their financial returns to themselves and their families.

Your Most Valuable Asset

Your most valuable financial asset is your *earning ability*, your ability to earn money. Properly applied to the marketplace, it's like a pump. By exploiting your earning ability, you can pump tens of thousands of dollars a year into your pocket. All your knowledge, education, skills and experience contribute toward your earning ability, which is your ability to get results for which someone will pay you good money.

Your earning ability is like farmland. If you don't take excellent care of it, if you don't fertilize it and cultivate it and water it on a regular basis, it soon loses its ability to produce the kind of harvest that you desire. Highly paid men and women are those who are extremely aware of the importance and value of their earning ability, and they work every day to keep it growing and current with the demands of the marketplace.

One of your greatest responsibilities in life is to identify, develop and maintain important marketable skills. It is to become very good at doing things for which there is a strong market demand.

What Are You Good at?

In corporate strategy, we call this the development of a "competitive advantage." For a company, a competitive advantage is defined as an *area of excellence* in producing a product or service that gives the company a distinct edge over its competition. This "unique added value" enables the company to charge premium prices for its products and services.

To earn what you are truly worth, as the president of your own personal services corporation, you also must have a clear competitive advantage. You also must have an area of excellence. You must be good at something, or several things, that makes you different from and better than your competitors. Your ability to identify and develop this competitive advantage is the most important thing you do in the world of work. This is the key to maintaining your earning ability. It's the foundation of your financial success. Without it, you're simply a pawn in a rapidly changing environment. But with a distinct competitive advantage, based on your strengths and abilities, you can write your own ticket. You can take charge of your own life. And the more distinct your competitive advantage, the more money you can earn and the more different ways in which you can earn it.

Think Strategically about Yourself

There are four keys to the strategic marketing of yourself and your services. These are applicable to huge companies such as General Motors, to candidates running for election and to individuals who want to accomplish the very most in the very shortest time.

The first of these four keys is *specialization*. No one can be all things to all people. A "jack-of-all-trades" also is a "master of none." That career path usually leads to a dead end. Specialization is the key. Men and women who are successful have a series of general skills, but they also have one or two areas where they have developed the ability to perform in an outstanding manner.

Think about the Future

Your decisions about how, where, when and why you are going to specialize in a particular area of endeavor are perhaps the most important decisions you will ever make in your career. The strategic planner, Michael Kami, once said that, "Those who do not think about the future cannot have one."

The major reason why so many people are seeing their jobs eliminated and finding themselves unemployed for long periods of time is because they didn't look down the road of life far enough and prepare themselves well enough for the time when their current jobs will expire. They suddenly found themselves out of gas on a lonely road, facing a long walk back to regular and well-paying employment. Don't let this happen to you.

In determining your area of specialization, put your current job aside for the moment, and take the time to look deeply into yourself. Analyze yourself from every point of view. Rise above yourself, and look at your lifetime of activities and accomplishments in determining what your area of specialization could be or should be.

Keep Your Mind Open

You might be doing exactly the right job for you at this moment. You might already be specializing in an important area where people are eager to pay you a lot of money for what you do. Your current work might be ideally suited to your likes and dislikes, to your temperament and your personality. Nevertheless, you owe it to yourself to be continually expanding the scope of your vision and looking toward the future to see where you might want to be in the months and years ahead. Remember, the best way to predict the future is to create it.

You possess special talents and abilities that make you unique, different from anyone else who has ever lived. The odds of there being another person just like you are more than 50 billion to one. Your remarkable combination of education, experiences, knowledge, problems, successes, difficulties and challenges, and your way of looking at and reacting to life, make you extraordinary.

You Have Unlimited Potential

You have within you, right now, potential competencies and

attributes that can enable you to accomplish virtually anything you want in life. Even if you lived for another 100 years, it would not be enough time for you to plumb the depths of your full potential. You will never be able to use more than a small part of your inborn abilities. Your main job is to decide which of your talents you are going to exploit and develop to their highest and best possible use right now.

What are you good at right now? If things continue as they are, what are you likely to be good at in the future—say one or two or even five years from now? Is this a marketable skill with a growing demand, or is your field changing in such a way that you are going to have to change as well if you want to keep up with it? Looking into the future, what *could* be your area of excellence if you were to go to work on yourself and your abilities? What *should* be your area of excellence if you want to rise to the top of your field, make an excellent living and take complete control of your financial future?

Keep Your Eyes Open

When I was 22, selling office supplies from business to business, I answered an advertisement for a copywriter for an advertising agency. As it happened, I had failed high-school English and I really had no idea what a copywriter did. I did not know that it was the person who wrote the advertising that appeared in print next to various pictures of products or services. I remember the executive who interviewed me and how nice he was at pointing out that I wasn't at all qualified for the job.

But something happened to me in the course of the interview process. The more I learned what was involved in the job, the more I thought about how much I would like to write advertising. And having been turned down flat during my first interview, I decided to learn more about the field.

Back to School

I went to the city library and began to check out and read books on advertising and copywriting. Over the next six months, while I worked at my regular sales job, I spent many hours devouring them. At the same time, I applied for copywriting jobs to advertising agencies in the city. I started with the small agencies first. When they turned me down, I asked them *why*? What was wrong with my application? What did I need to learn more about? What books would they recommend? And to this day, I remember that virtually everyone I spoke with was helpful to me.

By the end of six months, I had read every book on advertising and copywriting in the library and applied to every agency in the city, working up from the smallest agency to the very largest in the country. And by the time I had reached that level, I was ready. I was offered jobs as a junior copywriter by both the number-one and number-two agencies in the country. I took the job with the number-one agency and was very successful in a short period of time.

There Are No Limits

The point of this story is that I learned that you could become almost anything you needed to become, in order to accomplish almost anything you wanted to accomplish, if you simply decide what it is and then learn what you need to learn. This is such an obvious fact that most people miss it completely.

Some years later, I heard about a lot of people who had gotten into real estate development and made a lot of money. I decided that I wanted to get into real-estate development as well. I used my same strategy. I went to the library and began checking out and reading all the books on real-estate development that I could find. At that time, I had no money, no contacts and no knowledge of the industry. But I knew the great secret: I could learn what I needed to learn so that I could do what I wanted to do.

The Possibilities Are Endless

Within 12 months, I had tied up a piece of property with a $100 deposit and a 30-day option. I put together a proposal for a shopping center, as explained in the books. I tentatively approached several major potential anchor tenants and several minor tenants that together would take up 85 percent of the square footage I had proposed. Then I sold 75 percent of the entire package to a major development company in exchange for the company's putting up all the cash and providing me with the resources and people I needed to manage the construction of the shopping center and the completion of the leasing. Virtually everything that I did I had learned from books written by real-estate experts, books on the shelves of the local library.

The Same Principles Work

As you might have noticed, the fields of advertising and copywriting, and real-estate development, are very different. But these industries, and every business venture I have explored over the years, had one element in common. Success in each area was based on the decision, first, to specialize in that area and, second, to become extremely knowledgeable in that field so that I could do the work well if I got a chance.

In looking at your current and past experiences for an area of specialization, one of the most important questions to ask yourself is, "What activities have been most responsible for my success in life to date?"

How did you get from where you were to where you are today? What talents and abilities seemed to come easily to you? What things do you do well that seem to be difficult for most other people? What activities do you find most intrinsically motivating? What things make you happy when you are doing them?

Increase Your Earning Ability

In becoming more valuable, in increasing your ability to get results that people will pay you for, your level of interest, excitement and enthusiasm about the particular job or activity is a key factor. You'll always do best and make the most money in a field that you really enjoy. It will be an area that you like to think about and talk about and read about and learn about. Successful people love what they do, and they can hardly wait to get to it each day. Doing their work makes them happy, and the happier they are, the more enthusiastically they do it, and the better they do it as well.

Become Different and Better

The second key to becoming valuable is *differentiation*. You must decide what you're going to do to become not only different but also better than your competitors in the field. Remember, you have to be good in only one specific area to move ahead of the pack. And you must decide what that area should be. What do you, or could you, do better than almost anyone else?

Segment Your Market

The third strategic principle in developing resilience is *segmentation*. You have to look at the marketplace and determine where you can best apply yourself, with your unique talents and abilities, to give yourself the highest possible return on energy expended. What customers, companies, products, services or markets, can best utilize your special talents and offer you the most in terms of financial rewards and future opportunities?

Focus and Concentrate

The final key to personal strategic planning is *concentration*. Once you have decided the area in which you are going to specialize, how you are going to differentiate yourself, and where in the marketplace you can best apply your strengths, your final job is to concentrate all of your energy on becoming excellent in that extraordinary performance.

In the final analysis, everything that you have accomplished up to now is a part of the preparation for becoming outstanding in your chosen field. When you become very good at doing something that people want, need and are willing to pay for, you will soon begin moving rapidly into the top ranks of the highest paid people everywhere.

Become a Person of Influence

Albert Einstein, the great thinker and humanitarian, wrote that "You must teach men at the school of example, for they will learn at no other."

For you to become a person of influence, you must teach people how to become successful by selecting a field, a key skill, and then by becoming a big success, no matter how long it takes. As Theodore Roosevelt said, "Do what you can, with what you have, right where you are."

These are challenging times. But we have always had difficult times, times that develop your character, and bring out the best in you. Perhaps one of the most important lessons we learn in life is that you can only control your reactions to what happens to you. And in so controlling how you react and respond; you control the results of what happens. You take complete charge of your life.

Developing
Resilience in
Difficult Times

Author's Bio

Brian Tracy is Chairman and CEO of Brian

Tracy International, a company specializing in the training and development of individuals and organizations. He is among the top speakers, trainers, and seminar leaders in the world today.

Brian Tracy has consulted for more than 1,000 companies and addressed more than 5,000,000 people in 5,000 talks and seminars throughout the U.S., Canada and 82 other countries worldwide. As a keynote speaker and seminar leader, he addresses more than 250,000 people each year.

He has studied, researched, written, and spoken for 35 years in the fields of economics, history, business, philosophy and psychology. He is the top selling author of 80 books that have been translated into 42 languages.

Brian has written and produced more than 1000 audio and video learning programs, including the worldwide, best-selling Psychology of Achievement, which has been translated into 28 languages.

He speaks to corporate and public audiences on the subjects of personal and professional development, including the executives and staff of many of America's largest corporations. His exciting talks and seminars on Leadership, Sales, Self-Esteem, Goals, Strategy, Creativity and Success Psychology bring about immediate changes and long-term results. His "2-Day MBA" transforms business owners and companies.

Prior to founding his company, Brian Tracy International, Brian was the Chief Operating Officer of a $265 million dollar development company. He has had successful careers in sales and marketing, investments, real estate development and syndication, importation, distribution, and management consulting. He has conducted high level consulting assignments with several billion-dollar corporations in strategic planning and organizational development.

He has traveled and worked in 120 countries on six continents and speaks four languages. Brian is happily married and has four children. He is active in community and national affairs and is the President of three companies headquartered in San Diego, California.

Brian is the president of Brian Tracy International, an internet-based company that helps businesses of all sizes increase their sales and profitability by implementing the best practices of top businesses worldwide.

To learn more about Brian Tracy, please visit his website at:

🌐 www.briantracy.com

Believing Is Achieving

Strengthening Certain Skills in Achieving Success

Dr. Mehrdad Emadi

Believing Is Achieving
Strengthening Certain Skills in Achieving Success

Dr. Mehrdad Emadi

The First Experience

The first job does not always turn into success. My first experience in the job market failed. When I partnered with someone to distribute foodstuff during my time as an under-grad, I lost all my money because I blindly trusted my friend and didn't research the market. Afterwards, I didn't feel well for a few days, and I was gripped by a deep sense of despair. I felt like my world had been destroyed.

My family kept saying, "Why did you do this?" or "How could you trust him?" which made me feel even worse. I was in hell with no hope of getting out.

Privately, I considered whether "failure" was an appropriate categorization for such an event. This was the beginning of a success story. My first failure in starting a business taught me not to act impulsively without having the experience or necessary skills and without consulting anyone. A beautiful saying from Winston Churchill reads, "Success is the ability to go from one failure to another with no loss of enthusiasm."

After experiencing the first failure and accepting that I brought it on myself, I decided to get some experience before starting a second business. Working in my chosen field of water engineering, I began as an intern in a private company in Marvdasht in Fars province of Iran. The first few months were unpaid, and then I received my first paycheck. Because of this position, I was one of the active graduates in my professional field by the time my undergrad schooling ended.

As great minds like Pittacus Lore claim, "When you have lost hope, you have lost everything. And when you think all is lost, when all is dire and bleak, there is always hope."

The Second Experience

Given the experiences I gained working during my post-graduate studies, I established a privately held company in my professional field of water engineering after consulting others and taking extra care in the process.

Having already had one such experience, I thought I would not fail again. Nonetheless, I was ambitious, and my goal was to climb the ladder quickly, so I took on a major irrigation systems project. Since the employer was the government, payment was delayed for eight months, during which time I was hit with financial problems due to market fluctuations and not having enough money to cover the cheques I had issued.

I also experienced mental and psychological problems, once again, due to the stress I was feeling over my debt and being worried that my creditors would make me lose face in my workplace and neighborhood. I had to have an endoscopy and colonoscopy for a problem in my digestive system, and several doctors concluded that my digestive system was acting up due to the stress I was experiencing.

I endured the pain, took out a loan and sold my car. Financially, I was back at square one, but at least I found the money to cover the cheques I had issued, and this benefited my credit. I had a few terrible months with stress, insomnia, and horrific stomachaches. Yet, I was able to survive this crisis and change my circumstances by taking God's hand and nurturing my self-esteem, perseverance, and hopefulness.

When life turns tough, hope usually seems like a risk. We choose to have hope in things that might never happen, yet maybe circumstances will turn out as we desire. We need to accept despair and never give up hope. That is exactly what Georges Bernanos says when he claims, "Hope is a risk that must be run."

Nonetheless, life does not always go as planned.

The Third Experience

When I was working on my Ph.D., I made a new decision to start franchising, because I was in university full-time. I started two franchise branches in nearby towns. Once again, I faced financial problems due to being overly trusting and not consulting experts. My stress and digestive problems resurfaced, and I was troubled for some time. Thankfully, my previous experience allowed me to quickly wrap up the franchises and prevent too much severe financial tension.

Since I have always been optimistic about the future and interested in travelling, I applied for a tourist visa for Canada. After a few months, I was able to get a multi-entry five-year visa.

Given my professional and financial circumstances, my wife and I decided to have a month-long trip to Vancouver in 2019. We rented an apartment in downtown Vancouver on Georgia Street and began to experience new things. During the time we spent there, I talked to many Iranians and people of other nationalities who lived in Canada and had immigrated there a few years before. What interested me was that even though they were all away from their homeland, they had, knowingly or unknowingly, endured challenges that would help them strengthen their abilities. All were under circumstances of being away from family, living and working in a new environment, with a different climate, language, and culture. They had all chosen this path with absolute optimism, hoping that Canada would be much better for them, in the long run, than their previous country, and this optimism was essential to their success.

The Fourth Experience

A few months after returning from Canada, there was a new change in my life: the birth of a child. Despite the increase in responsibilities, fatherhood brought me joy. I had to commute 70 km to Shiraz for work and administrative tasks most days of the week. I decided to move to Shiraz because my wife needed me more now. This was a new decision for me and brought with it the challenges of renting a home, renting an office, and affording day-to-day costs. This decision also set the horizon for my family's future. I tried harder to overcome the challenges, and absolute optimism was my guide.

A few months after having moved to Shiraz, I was browsing through available work applications, while trying to get a guarantor for the bank to participate in the bidding. When I opened one application, I saw an ad that a workshop producing drip irrigation equipment relevant to my expertise was up for sale. I called them and set up a face-to-face meeting with their executive manager to visit the workshop. When the owner realized that I was an expert in the field of irrigation and an energetic young person eager to work, he welcomed me enthusiastically.

In addition to being optimistic and believing tomorrow was better than today, this time I consulted people and my risk-taking came to be my advantage. Although I needed a large sum of money, I relied on God, and my faith convinced my subconscious self that I would be able to get the money. We signed a contract, and I bought the workshop with a 10% down payment.

I started my work relying on God, and I was able to expand

Mirab Kala and establish some exclusive franchises across the province. I also expanded our field of specialty from agriculture to include construction. I was able to launch our online sales platform www.mirabkala.ir and be more active on Instagram. Eventually, I succeeded in reviving the Mirab Kala brand in production of Shabnam, IES, or Sam Etesalat equipment and the supply of irrigation equipment generally.

Personal Development on the Path to Success

Since I was interested in education and had gained some experience, I pursued educational investments. I also decided to take part in a course on success taught by a famous Iranian professor. This was the beginning of my personal development journey. I was introduced to an educational organization in Tehran by my new friends and started training in business coaching. So far, I have taken several online and in-person courses for personal growth. I have become more successful in my business, while learning that I can help others by understanding what happened to me and how I was able to deal with my failures and achieve success. I decided to create a personal website and use Instagram to help others, as much as I could, to achieve success.

If I had felt frozen by fear at the start when I faced rough times, if I had not trusted myself to be adaptable, I would be someone else's employee, like so many of my friends who started working at the same time I did. I wouldn't have progressed financially, professionally, and spiritually, and I would still feel regretful about the lost times and the success I could have enjoyed.

We need to believe we can achieve what we desire and aim for by not giving up in the face of difficulties. This attitude has several components:

1. **Hope**. As wise men like Pablo Neruda assert, the human capacity to be hopeful is the most wonderful truth in life. Hope determines a clear destination for human-kind and gives them the energy to start. We must be hope-ful that we have a better life in future, just as others are hopeful that they can create a better future.

2. **Helpfulness.** If we can do something for others, we must, even if it is only sending a good vibe. I have come to believe that just as I help others without expecting anything, others have given me a hand and helped me achieve more success. Beethoven said if you want to be prosperous in life, work for others' prosperity, because the happiness we give others returns to our hearts.

3. **Responsibility.** We need to be committed and take responsibility for whatever we do, whether the result is good or bad, because being responsible improves our ability and growth.

4. **Patience**. We need to work on our patience and give ourselves time to achieve our goal. It is with patience that

we achieve success. If I had not been patient from the beginning, perhaps I would not be in the position I am in my field after ten years. "You can create beautiful things out of the obstacles on your way." (Erich Kastner, German author)

5. **Perseverance**. Try to always persevere because when you do not, the desired outcome will not be realized, due to delays and loss of motivation. We might get nothing if we walk out halfway. "Selecting a goal and sticking to it can change everything."[1]

6. **Motivation**. We have all had challenges and overcome them successfully. Our successes might be small in size, but we can encourage ourselves to take bigger steps by reviewing them. A swift and powerful leopard can never fly even if she runs at 1000 km/hr, because we need wings to fly, not swiftness and strength. As humans, our wings are our mind. Success has nothing to do with our body shape, beauty, gender, strength, age, or nationality; the rate of our success relies on the way we use our minds. As Rumi put it, "the way to the sky is from within. You need to use the wings of love. When your wings of love are strengthened enough, there will be no need for a ladder."

7. **Self-improvement.** We should always work on our mind and our thoughts. Just as our body needs food for fuel, our mind and soul need nourishment that comes

---

[1]   Scott Reed

from books, educational videos, and training classes.

8. **Positivity**. The mind is sensitive, so it is important that we give ourselves the signal that positive changes are on the way. When we interact with positive people, they make us have a greater motivation for success and help us have a smooth ride with their positive vibes. Our thoughts are energy; they are powerful and creative. Our thoughts directly affect our behavior. We can adjust our behavior by making our thoughts more positive.

9. **Appreciation**. People who thank God sincerely for what they have in mind have true faith. They will be rich and able to provide the necessities to create whatever they desire. Friedrich Nietzsche claimed that the essence of all elegant and excellent art is appreciation. Joseph Edison believes there is no deed more pleasant for the mind than appreciation; this act brings with itself such internal contentment that can only be rewarded by performing our duty.

Most of us face challenges in life that we can overcome with the help of education and improving our existing potentials of faith, hope, positivity, feeling good, etc. These empower us to endure and persevere in critical conditions, to have patience and increase our capacity to feel more empowered and achieve success. This is one of the main pillars of self-sufficiency: to be able to overcome a crisis and achieve the success we have in mind.

Given my own experiences, and the teachings of the respected professor Dr. Shahab Anari, we can improve our ability to successfully overcome difficult situations by learning the skills of resilience.

Resilience is a combination of seven micro-skills:

1- Adjusting emotions

2- Controlling impulses

3- Absolute optimism

4- Analyzing the root causes

5- Empathy

6- Self-sufficiency

7- Seeking new experiences

I hope I have been able to take a small step in helping you achieve success. I will end with a quote from Dr Anari: "Resilience is a skill that can be learned when we believe people can change."

God bless you.

Believing Is Achieving
Strengthening Certain Skills in Achieving Success

Author's Bio

Dr. Mehrdad Emadi helps his audience

walk an easier path towards their goals with his academic teachings.

When he began his studies in the field of water engineering in 2011, his professors always told Mehrdad that he was a persistent and determined person who will accomplish great things in the future.

Mehrdad is an entrepreneur and the founder of *Mirab Kala*. He regularly gives talks on topics of personal growth and business development. He has also been the manager of the contracting company *Geeti Negar Newsaad* which works in

Iran in areas relevant to water.

Mehrdad has published ten articles in domestic and international journals, and he is the translator of the best-selling book *Good time-Also success* in Iran.

He started practicing the kyokushin karate in 2008, and he is currently a coach in this sport with a dan 2.

He received his Master's in Water Engineering in 2012 with a grade point average of 19.18 (out of 20).

Mehrdad annually provides novel irrigation systems equipment for approximately 70 million square meters of agricultural land by producing and supplying droppers from *Shabnam, IES,* and *Sam Ettesalat,* which will lead to saving a huge amount of water.

Mehrdad has been helping people to have better lives and better incomes for over ten years, and he has increased his social media presence since the pandemic began. Currently, Persian-speaking people all around the world use his consultations, talks, and videos.

Mehrdad also volunteers quite a lot. He works to improve the use of water and increase water conservation and efficiency as a member of the Water Engineering Association's executive board. He acts as consultant and supplier on projects related to underdeveloped areas of Iran, including Sistan and Baloochestan.

Mehrdad is always learning and educating himself, and he is constantly thankful to God. He also has a beautiful son named Mehrsam and is blessed to have married his wife, Maryam.

You can contact him at:

✉ Mehrdad_e73@yahoo.com

🌐 www.mehrdademadi.ir

📷 www.instagram.com/Dr.mehrdademadi/

📷 www.instagram.com/Mirabkala/

🌐 www.mirabkala.ir

Challenging Ourselves
Training the Brain
to Take Action

Pegah Ghiasian

Challenging Ourselves
Training the Brain to Take Action

Pegah Ghiasian

When I was close to graduating from university in computer engineering, I struggled with many problems. I felt there was something missing from my life, a feeling that was not normal, and I could no longer control the sensation. Though I did not know what the origin of this feeling was, I knew my current way of life was not very satisfying to me.

At that point in time, I was working for my father's company and as a remote employee for a telecommunications company. In my father's construction company, I oversaw setting up the data and providing interior and exterior designs with AutoCAD, 3DS Max, and Lumion software. For the telecommunications company, I designed websites as project works.

Then, when I experienced a humiliating failure, I decided to get out of my comfort zone and try to progress in a new direction.

The Challenge of New Experiences

Enrolling in the Nokhbegan Marketing and Entrepreneurship Institute, I took a variety of courses related to developing confidence and self-esteem, negotiation techniques, sales and marketing of a product or service, principles of strategic management, contract law, and tax rules.

When in the process of learning pleasant things, dopamine is released, and motivation is boosted. At first, learning was especially delightful for me. But when doing difficult work, my brain grew tired, and I experienced exhaustion. Nonetheless, I always tried to maintain my initial motivation.

Having Willpower and Determination, Not Mere Motivation

Despite all the difficulties this new path presented for me, I made so much progress that one of the institute's professors asked me in front of all the learners to help their sales team as well as to improve their website. I did not know why he offered me this opportunity. Now that I think clearly about it, I can recognize that I did not have anything special compared to other learners except my level of determination. I do not say *motivation,* because that may end at some point. My unique trait was that I constantly persisted, even in times of fatigue and confusion, and my colleagues could sense my learning endurance. In fact, it was a great success for me that such a reliable and specialized institute acknowledged and offered me such a proposal, in front of all the other learners, without any request from me.

Finding Areas of Interest

Where was my greatest interest? Direct contact with people made me feel good. Most importantly, being able to make an effective contribution to improve people's quality of life and help them to be happy increased my own feelings of self-worth. Here, I felt that my purpose in life was more than just working.

Walk the Path without Self-judgment and Limiting Beliefs

I recognized that I was not created for mere administrative and technical work. Although I still had a fear of failure, I knew for certain that my personality was of a social type. To grow, I had to come out of my current working paradigm and take on a new form. Hence, I made friends with many students in the same institute. These contacts also believed what mattered most was honesty and a genuine desire to be of help to others. Even if a product or service would be less profitable for me but more beneficial to others, I preferred to help them solve their problem.

Motivation and Determination Based on Pragmatism

I was not very interested in inspirational speeches and usually found them unconvincing, because I knew the short-term effects of dopamine. Instead, I looked for scientific methods that worked well, even when I struggled with difficult situations.

I wanted to take a step further and become a more active learner, so I turned to self-awareness courses and subsequently became very interested in them. As a starter, I focused on Jung's books and spent some time reading them. My broadening interests inspired me to think about all aspects of life in addition to my former field of expertise.

I recommend to others that taking steps such as I did should be done gradually, because it is very difficult to manage several heavy tasks at the same time. Sometimes it may not be possible to juggle the pursuit of multiple interests at once, because it's necessary to concentrate on one important area and prevent the possibility of low-quality work.

Though I had a special feeling after studying Jung's books, I was somewhat confused and felt the need to relax my mind and take care of my body.

Taking Care of Body and Health with Mindful Self-compassion

I took tennis and fitness courses, gradually became more interested in them, and received a fitness coaching certificate. At the same time, I did a ten-minute meditation every day and relaxed my mind.

Being a busy person, I found that meditation helped me considerably to concentrate effectively on my activities and have a clearly coherent mind. I also practiced creating small joys and celebrations for myself, after reading Stephen Guise's book entitled *Mini Habits: Smaller Habits, Bigger Results*. Guise recommends taking small steps to build big habits. Following this advice, I soon saw the effects of happiness, even small joys, on my mind.

It occurred to me that overeating is sometimes unconsciously considered a reward for the brain, causing the secretion of hormones. We can realize we have no need for this behavior when we consciously retool our brains and reduce or eliminate overeating.

Then, another idea came along. Due to my interest and experience in design and my preference to make people happy, one of my friends suggested that we might start cooperatively making decorations for all kinds of celebrations. We could thereby have a share in people's happiness as an important element of a happy human life. Accordingly, the topday4u group was formed.

Refusal to Accept Limiting Beliefs

It has always been interesting to me that, unlike people who cannot financially afford to realize some of their dreams, there are also people who are relatively prosperous but do not have the courage and belief in making more progress. They experience stagnation because they have limiting beliefs influenced by many factors, including early childhood experiences.

It is not enough merely to be interested in progress, you must work hard, move along the path, and consistently gain experience. To do this, you need to give yourself the opportunity and this requires self-kindness above all. You may think unconsciously that you should not fail because doing so, your destiny and reputation will be affected! This indicates that not only do you suffer from fears but that you also cannot manage them. They limit your mind and do not allow it to go beyond its present perspective, because you think that doing so will not have good results and you will be judged poorly.

It is clear this is not an ideal way of thinking. No one can be proficient in a pursuit from its beginning, except in a few rare cases. A part of the brain called the reptilian brain constantly tricks you into staying in your comfort zone and not pursuing new and unfamiliar paths. However, science has demonstrated there is no such thing as an inability to learn or a lack of talent being a barrier. It can only be said that the neural pathway for performance of a new task has not yet been formed in the brain!

The brain has the same requirement as the muscles: it needs to be trained. Neuroscience points out there are about 85 billion neurons in the brain and each neuron can have 10,000 connections with other neurons. These connections are designed to learn and can only be enhanced by practice. Thus, if you do not utilize your brain functions optimally, you lose them.

I think the Law of Attraction has a missing link: you get everything by *paying its costs*. As Aaron Balik states, "Fear should only be accepted," and we should not be stopped by it at all. According to Brian Tracy, from whom I am always learning, only twenty percent of the community is willing to learn and grow continuously. Therefore, it is your choice to be dynamic or live statically.

Finally, I finish my words with verses of Saadi, as follows:

Nobility is not all about giving speeches.

Actions speak louder than words.

Challenging
Ourselves
Training
the Brain to Take
Action

Author's Bio

Pegah Ghiasian graduated in computer engineering and gained experience in design and decoration, agency representation, business branding, increasing sales and conversion rates in digital marketing, and website design, all of which have enhanced personal growth and development as well as helping companies to experience real and honest growth in their business.

Contact Pegah at:

🌐 www.pegahghiasian.com
🅂 Pegah Ghiasian
📷 Pegahghn

of *Ashes* and *Hopes*
How I Became a Serial
Entrepreneur

Raghwa Gopal

Of Ashes and Hopes
How I Became a Serial Entrepreneur

Raghwa Gopal

The adjacent building was ablaze, and so were my dreams. Nevertheless, out of the ashes may begin a new life once more. Over and over again, I went through the story of how years of hard work had burned to the ground. Every minutiae of that incident and the terrible moments of the days that came after were visibly clear in my mind's eye. But now, it was time to think ahead and never look back again.

Prologue

In 1979, I set foot in Canada to find new opportunities for building a business. A young man of 20, I did not have many resources, and any venture would entail high levels of risk for me. As a software developer, I had to find opportunities for work in a city where there were not many such openings. However, I was lucky enough to have met a man who was in the software business, and he provided me with the opportunity of my life, to be in this business.

I was a high-achiever, and I put my heart and soul into the work, so the outcome could turn out to be a shining one. The man came in one day and told me that my work was second to none, hence he wanted to make me a partner in the business.

It was a golden opportunity for anyone who had the money to buy half of the company, but I was not that person. I had come to this town from Fiji with only 300 dollars in my pocket, and I had just started to work. I had to support my family here and my family back in Fiji; therefore, I did not possess the means to capitalize on that opportunity.

Nevertheless, I had a keen interest in partnering with him, so I told him about all the money I had saved up to that moment. It was not sufficient, but I could also borrow some money from the bank to make up for a portion of the deficit. Still, I would need more money. He agreed to lend me the remaining amount and told me that I was so great at my job that he would do anything to make me his partner.

The business was booming until the adjacent building caught fire and it spread to our building. Everything was obliterated. At moments like this, people lose the ability to think and make rational decisions. With the backup of our software, we could run the business again. But for that, we needed time and monetary compensation. It was such a dilemma, because the business was not insured properly, and it would take a long time and passing through lots of complicated stages for us to receive assistance from the insurance company.

After three weeks, we finally managed to secure a new system and download the backup files, which gave me some comfort. However, I realized that I needed to invest more money in the business because my initial investment was not sufficient for me to be able to afford insurance. The word got out, and the companies we were competing with started to take advantage of the fact that we were, at least temporarily, out of business.

There were some rays of hope coming from unforeseen sources, ones I could not see at the time because my mind was wrestling with an adverse train of thoughts, disillusion and hopelessness. For instance, we had a great customer who presented us with a kind offer of help. He told us we could use his office and equipment, and he would also help us with the insurance processes and customer-related issues. However, the problem was not yet to be solved, because a significant number of our customers were worried about their projects. We needed more time to recover and get everything going again. We talked to them about why they should trust us and why they should stay with us. In fact, all of them did stay with us. But we lost some potential future customers due to the badmouthing our competitors had started against us.

This predicament was a greatly unfortunate event, because I had spent years working hard to build our current status, and now it was all gone. I was so confused and needed to consult my mentor, the person who had always given me invaluable advice in life.

The Peripeteia

My mentor, a distant relative whom I have at times relied

upon for sound advice, listened to me intently. I talked for a long time about what had happened, how I had lost everything and had gotten myself in debt for the rest of my life. Having listened to all I had to say, he asked me to go home and review what had happened in my head. Perhaps even several times. And then, I was to think about what I would do to solve this, never and under no circumstances looking back to past events. Despite its simplicity, I found this a great piece of advice when I followed it. In fact, it cost me very little time and gave me so much clarity of mind.

In an interesting turn of events, my customers showed incredible generosity and kindness to provide me with the time and help I needed. This kindness had its roots in my decision to be completely authentic and genuine. I was honest with every single customer, so, instead of not telling them exactly what had happened, I did the opposite.

I talked to one customer and told him about the dire situation we were in. To my surprise, he identified with me, offering me all he could do to help. I went to the second customer, and the response was equally sympathetic. So I went to every customer we had with the story of our challenging situation, and all of them were amazingly cooperative. They were so kind that, in addition to giving us time to fulfill our commitments, they also offered to help us get back on our feet by providing the money in advance and the equipment we needed.

The effect of my authentic approach and honest attitude was so profound that some of them became my friends, even lifelong friends, and we managed to cultivate relationships beyond that of just a businessman and his customer. It was unveiled to me just how influential authenticity and genuineness could be in the path towards one's accomplishments.

An invaluable lesson I learned in the face of adversity was the immense utility of being connected to a network of people in my community so I could reach out to them when I needed help. I always tell the younger generation, and to anyone who needs advice, to have a relationship with someone who has been through life, has lots of experience and has seen things you have not. Though these people may not be able to give you any advice, if they can, it will be golden. Even if they do not provide you with advice, just speaking to them will enable you to achieve more clarity and find solutions on your own.

People ask me, "Where can we find these folks?" I know there are lots of individuals, communities, and organizations out there who will provide such mentoring services. However, my advice is to go with someone with whom you have a continuous and deep relationship, business-wise or life-wise. It could be your lawyer or accountant, or even someone among your relatives. They can help you overcome things that you may not be able to resolve if left to your own devices. For example, your lawyer may provide you with insights into the legal aspects of your struggle. Your accountant may be able to guide you through the maze of complicated monetary and non-monetary regulations involved in a financial issue with the bank or insurance. Whatever your struggle is, do not go it alone.

The Longings of a Serial Entrepreneur

So what happened after the business was wiped out? The first three weeks were horrible. The next three or four weeks were better but still stressful. My business partner and I managed to buy another building with a small down payment. After that, the business was ultra-successful. The fire incident took place in 1987. By 2001, when we sold the business, we were one of the most successful software suppliers to local governments and companies, with over 100 people working for us. Indeed, we were one of the largest businesses in our line of work in both Canada and the U.S.

I had saved enough money to retire and go back to the paradise that was Fiji. Nevertheless, I became bored out of my mind by not working. Even the people with whom I played golf were talking about their work issues. So, I invested in another company. It rapidly proliferated and was sold in 2006. I did this repeatedly with a number of other companies until 2009, when the last business was sold and I decided not to grow startups and businesses anymore.

I now had a desire to engage in not-for-profit work to benefit the community, for instance, helping at the YMCA,

United Way and Project Literacy. I wanted to provide my services to whoever needed them, mostly by providing education to those who were deprived of it. I also became an advisor at the University of British Columbia (UBC) to provide mentorship to the students. They come to me with all kinds of issues, from how to build and run a startup to life issues that prove challenging to them. I have been doing this for the last fifteen years or so.

At the same time, I started to build a technology ecosystem in the region of Okanagan, British Columbia. The primary rationale behind this decision was that there was no such company there when we established ours in 1979, and it was challenging to find and hire new people. Hence, if there were more companies, the interchange of people could be facilitated. The tech ecosystem turned into a marvelously large one, the fastest growing in North America. It had one company in 1979 with almost 60 people, and today it features over 1000 companies with more than 15,000 employees, delivering an annual economic impact of nearly two billion dollars. I serve on numerous boards now, including as co-Vice-Chair of UBC's Board of Governors. Most of the boards I am on are related to entities that do not-for-profit work. In fact, doing philanthropic work is a priority in my family.

Right now, I serve as the President and CEO of Innovate BC, which is part of the provincial government of British

Columbia. We support and promote innovation in all sectors and all regions of the province. Moreover, I envision our future to include world-class work that is recognized around the globe. Once that is done, I will be totally retired and focused on two things. First, I will devote considerable time to our family foundation to do even more philanthropic work, and second, I will be around to help not-for-profit entities which need and can benefit from my help.

There is one thing always on my mind when I wake up and when I go to bed: I am a very fortunate person. Lots of people helped me throughout my life, and I will never forget that. I will do the same for other people until the last moment of my life.

Of Ashes and
Hopes
How I Became
a Serial
Entrepreneur

Author's Bio

A serial entrepreneur who has extensive experience starting, growing and selling numerous businesses, **Raghwa Gopal** recently joined Innovate BC from Accelerate Okanagan (AO), where he was CEO. At AO, Gopal was instrumental in the creation and management of successful programs for technology companies at all stages of growth, and he has been a driving force in the development of the Okanagan's tech sector into a $1.6 billion economic contributor.

A graduate of New Zealand's Central Institute of Technology in information technology, Raghwa has also received diplomas in computer science from Australia's Collier MacMillan School.

In addition to his corporate experience, Gopal has lectured in the Faculty of Management (Business) at UBC Okanagan and the School of Arts and Sciences (Computer Science); has been an Entrepreneur-in-Residence at Okanagan College School of Business; and serves on the boards of multiple organizations, including as a member of the Board of Governors for University of British Columbia and India Canada Innovation Council. He has also served as a member of BC RCMP's Diversity and Inclusion Board and is a current member of Greater Vancouver Board of Trade's Diversity and Inclusion Leadership Council.

To learn more about Raghwa or to connect, head to:

🌐 RaghwaGopal.com

Resilience
Is the "R" in Rise
A Life Lesson from My Beloved Parents

Elisabeth Kibitek Goueth

Resilience Is the "R" in Rise
A Life Lesson from My Beloved Parents

Elisabeth Kibitek Goueth

How It All Started: An Entrepreneur's Journey

With shaky hands and teary eyes, she took the National Agricultural Excellence Award of the Year. She still couldn't believe it. She stared at the assembly of distinguished public servants, traditional and religious authorities, as well as representatives of renowned international organizations.

Little Elissa had just made history in her region. She had beaten all the odds. Who could have predicted such an achievement? Less than five years ago, she was still an unknown girl, deprived of affection and raised by strangers. Having been mistreated, she had always felt like an intruder, and loneliness had been her cup of tea for years. The uncertainty of tomorrow and a lack of self-confidence were her faithful companions for as long as she could remember.

She had no one to share her dreams, her desires or even her fears with. She kept it all buried deep inside her. She dreamed of becoming a great businesswoman, and always knew that she would have to work extremely hard to get there. In fact, at every stage of her life, only her unwavering determination saved her. And that's exactly what made her shine on this day,

71

a determination sustained by the passion to improve her life and get rid of the emptiness and uncertainties she dragged along since childhood.

Her tearful gaze swept over the crowd once again and landed on Roger, her husband. She was moved as she was remembering the times when they were first dating. Everything had happened so fast. He offered her his genuine love and enlivened her self-confidence, thanks to his unfailing support and generous encouragements. He revealed the brave woman she had become since their marriage three years ago.

She remembered their conversation the very first day of their journey into business. It was a beautiful sunny afternoon with a cool breeze, reminiscent of the torrential rain of the day before. They went to **Nkong-Bôdôl** the estate they had recently acquired. Everything remained to be done there. The forest was still overpowering. Holding hands, they talked about the best way to develop the area. Roger was eager to launch a processing plant, but the project was so ambitious that it would take them several years to raise the initial capital.

Inhaling the scent of the earth after the rain, carried by the wind, she had a revelation. Suddenly, she was seized by the desire to connect with the land, a passion passed on to her by her beloved late grandmother. She stared at Roger and said, "What do you think about keeping things simple? We can start with a smaller project that would allow us to tame this land while making money at the same time. I know we lack the money we need to start our larger project. Why not grow some food crops first and sell them? I'm pretty sure we can work wonders here."

He looked at her, amused, and said, "It will still take us forever to get there. And we will have to overcome the same challenges."

Not convinced by his arguments, she replied, "You know, darling, the earth never lies. I am sure that if we start with a field of 500 square meters, next year we will do better."

"And what will you do with the remaining twenty hectares?" he retorted.

"Let's try before giving up. I promise you, if the revenue from the first harvest doesn't balance at least all the expenses, I'll stop everything."

"And how will you cope with your current teaching job? Farming is tricky, filled with so many unknowns. You're not even sure the soil is fertile, or whether the seeds you want to use are of the best quality. I think you have to be a specialist to take on such a project."

"I'll find a way! My grandmother didn't study for this," she added with a smile.

As she smiled, several feelings took her over. Ever ready for a challenge, she felt lost and didn't really know where to start. She remembered her grandmother used to say, "When you get inspired and you feel it in your soul, then know that Mother

Nature is speaking to you. Go ahead, work on the idea, and make it feasible while considering your situation and your means. Avoid sticking only to the first plan, however beautiful it may seem. Dig deeper and deeper to find the right way."

She then decided to follow her grandmother's advice. She was obsessed with the smell of the earth and wanted to inhale it again, but with a smile of success. She began by figuring out the types of seeds that matched the actual planting season. She visited food markets and used the opportunity of a purchase to engage the sellers in conversations about their supply channels. One thing leading to another, she managed to contact their seed producers and gather lots of useful advice.

That first year, she only managed to farm 250 square meters of land. To add to that, the harvest was very poor. She was frustrated and ashamed of losing her challenge, despite her strong commitment. Her old fears were coming back to haunt her. Confiding in her husband, he just asked her one question, "Did you enjoy investing in and working on this land?"

She nodded, "Yeah, very much! It brought back happy memories. You know, I just have a few. Besides, I made a lot of acquaintances. I learned a lot. That's why I don't understand the poor outcome."

He tenderly took her in his arms and said, "I too learned a lot from this adventure. You had important losses as well as dozens of gains. Consider this year as a learning experience and start over. I'm sure you'll perform better next time. The crops are from good quality stock, and the results are amazingly tasty. Maybe we should contact the farmers' organizations to learn more about the processes involved in farming such crops. I encourage you to continue. Your efforts will pay off. Sometimes you need patience. Farming is not my primary passion, but I'm up for helping you whenever you need it."

Her eyes were wide open as she was listening to him. His words filled her with enthusiasm. She was so grateful. "Thank you very much. You're right, I will continue. But I think I should change the type of food I'm growing."

In the second year, Elissa participated in multiple training courses offered through government programs. This time, the yield was satisfactory. Although expenses increased, the quality of the crops from her 500 square meter farm was enough to fuel her satisfaction.

In a conversation with one of her clients, she learned about a contest organized by the Ministry of Agriculture to encourage farm owners and spark more interest in food farming.

Thanks to Roger and the genuine appreciation of her customers, she decided to enter the contest. Emboldened by her past experiences, she targeted a two-hectare area for her new farm, and carefully planned everything (labour, use of fertilizers, watering systems, etc.). She had even quit her teaching job to focus solely on farming. Although the results this time exceeded her expectations, she couldn't imagine winning the national award. For her, the best prize was her ability to push her limits and take risks.

Now, here she was, standing in front of an admiring audience, patiently awaiting her speech. As she spoke that day, she felt grateful for life once again. Without realizing it, the hardships of her whole life had shaped her and somehow prepared her for this moment. The pride in her husband's eyes, the admiration of the other contestants and the respect of the authorities were priceless. She told herself "Game over! Ready for the next round."

What's in It for Me and You?

Elissa and Roger, whose amazing entrepreneurial experience has just been narrated, are my dear parents. Their lives have always been a source of inspiration for me.

As women, wives, mothers, immigrants and people from visible minorities, our professional choices are often driven by our desire to protect our loved ones from precarious and uncertain situations. The constraints of these five terms which I call the $5D^2$ generally tend to wipe out our dreams and entrepreneurial passion, forcing many into low-wage employment. Identifying as a 5D woman, I made the challenging choice to get into the world of entrepreneurship.

---

2   The "5 Dimensions" refers to people with specific challenges: women, married, mothers, immigrants, and visible minorities.

A Bamileke[3] proverb says: "The calabash[4] of a lucky man always grows in the bush." This means if someone wants to succeed, they should roll up their sleeves and work to unlock the success that lies behind all the constraints. In fact, do not dwell on the obstacles, but know how to deal with them to reach your goals.

The story of my parents, and especially of my mother, is always a source of timeless lessons, interesting for entrepreneurs and even more for 5D women.

Here are the nine lessons my parents' business story taught me about entrepreneurship:

1. Passion must be one of the pillars of our desire to get into entrepreneurship. We should engage in activities we are passionate about, or else work to become passionate about them, to avoid losing interest when faced with challenging times.

2. Self-confidence is crucial. It drives involvement, allows one to better manage difficulties ahead and to accept failures. Besides, doesn't FAIL commonly refers to First Attempt In Learning[5]?

---

3   An ethnic group from Cameroon in Central Africa, whose people are known for their business and entrepreneurial spirit.

4   Calabashes are large dry fruits that can be used as containers of various objects. https://fr.wikipedia.org/wiki/Calabash.

5   Dr. A.P.J. Abdul Kalam (1931-2015), engineer, scientist, author, professor, and politician (11th president of India):"If you fail, never give up because FAIL means "First Attempt In Learning".

3. Learn to face questions, obstacles, and contradictions. These provide the means for improvement and risk anticipation.

4. Our vision must be limitless and our actions pragmatic and realistic. Don't just rely on forecasts, often as large as our vision. Instead, focus on feasibility.

5. Alone we can go fast, but with others, we can go the distance. Internal motivation is not always enough. We need to be challenged on our decisions, have interactions with others and receive their feedback. Trustworthy people are equally as important as opponents. Here is a popular saying: "Ask your enemy for advice and do the opposite of what they tell you."

6. Diversify partnerships and nurture relationships. Never burn a bridge because you never know where the key is hidden. Often, it's the people we suspect the least who can save us from our predicaments.

7. Keep learning and be open-minded. Good ideas are not proven skills. Also, don't give up on ideas because you don't know anything about a specific field. Investing time and money to acquire the necessary knowledge is one of the guarantees of success.

8. Having role models helps us build our perspectives and strategies. They help us shape our vision.

9. Support from our loved ones is the driving force behind everything we do. Therefore, support must be consistent.

Final Thoughts

So many good words, we might think. But what are they worth without actions? My father used to say, "Whatever the situation, actions not words are most valuable. Stay focused and persevere!"

I am committed to taking actions according to the lessons I've learned over the years. That's why when I came to Canada, I chose to follow my passion. Onetwo Consulting has crossed continents, and slowly but steadily continues to impact businesses and people. Kiafrik[6] is on the way. Other projects are in the pipelines.

- Is it easy? I must manage daily challenges.
- Have I reached my destination? I am just starting the journey.
- Do I feel discouraged? Sometimes.
- Will I give up? Never!

5D women, I leave you with this inspiring piece of advice from my mother: "A woman with a job is an independent woman, and as such is able to significantly contribute to her home and to society's development in countless ways."

---

6   A culture-related online store.

*Resilience Is the
"R" in Rise*
*A Life Lesson from
My Beloved Parents*

Author's Bio

Elisabeth Kibitek Goueth is a Registered Professional Trainer in Canada. She has been working in the banking industry since 2007, mostly in Africa. After a successful career in Learning and Development, Alternative Delivery Channels and Sales, she decided to pursue her dreams of working independently. She then established herself as a consultant in Training and Digital Finance, operating in developing countries.

Being an entrepreneur at heart, she relocated her services to the Greater Toronto Area when she moved to Canada with Onetwo Consulting, a firm specializing in Learning and

Development, Risk Management and Customer Service, both in English and French.

Elisabeth is passionate about helping people achieve their goals and finds it most rewarding to promote others' well-being and success. Through her consultancy services, she is committed to providing unique interventions that help individuals and organizations reach their goals in a seamless and rigorous manner while applying the latest principles in Project Management.

Thanks to her outstanding adaptability and determination, Elisabeth is launching a culture-related online store specializing in promoting multiculturalism and eco-friendly products. Her purpose is to motivate people to take advantage of their own culture and integrate it into the Canadian environment to benefit from the best of both worlds. She also encourages everyone to fearlessly embrace cultural diversity and endorse the fight for a clean environment.

Elisabeth is happily married to her business partner Francis and is the proud mother of three handsome subject matter experts for children's books, Francis Jr., Elvyn and Akil. She can be reached at:

🌐 www.onetwoconsulting.com
🌐 www.kiafrik.com
in www.linkedin.com/in/elisabeth-kg

Never Stop Dreaming, Never Assume

Always Keep Listening and Learning

Liza Jones

Never Stop Dreaming, Never Assume Always Keep Listening and Learning

Liza Jones

Attending 15 schools, coupled with undiagnosed dyslexia, has given me several advantages and disadvantages. I developed the ability to rapidly change, be flexible and see other people's perspectives. But I was usually the new girl, and as such, found it difficult to make friends. So, I became resilient, acquiring the strength needed to adapt well and bounce back quickly in times of upheaval and uncertainty.

In business, the road is often paved with periods of emotional stress, but by developing resilience, you will be able to keep things in balance, maintain positive mental health and handle the challenges confronting you. You will be stronger in the face of adversity.

So come with me and discover why you should never stop dreaming, never assume, always keep listening and learning. The door to business and personal success is not far away.

Old Maids Teaching

With countless potential husbands killed in the War, and so little prospect of marriage, many spinsters in the 1950s and 1960s became teachers, devoting their lives to educating the next generation. Often applying rigid Victorian standards, they instilled in me a love of learning for its own sake.

They prepared pupils for adult female life in the late 20th century. With a longer-term perspective, the options for careers for middle-class girls were to become a secretary, teacher, nurse or something similar, and if lucky, you might secure a company director or a doctor as a husband. In the event, I married an actuary, but more about that later.

My father's career as a dental surgeon and lecturer meant we regularly moved house, so although my loving parents were very keen on education, I was rarely in any one school for long. One year I went to three different schools, and the standards and curricula at each school varied. I excelled at subjects like mathematics and the sciences but was often in trouble for being too talkative. Perhaps I was attention-seeking. Nonetheless, I was building the adaptability needed to thrive when facing life's problems.

I started earning pocket money on Saturdays at the age of fourteen, working in retail, quickly learning customer service techniques and budgeting. This was a great way to develop skills in dealing with a wide range of people.

A Double Somersault

After training as a science teacher, I started work one September and returned home to my parents at the end of that first term. I borrowed my mother's car on Christmas Eve and promptly turned it over in a double somersault by falling asleep at the wheel. Sometimes things just happen.

Not one to be overwhelmed by such trauma, I used the healing months of convalescence to reappraise my true goals. I wanted to travel, to see other cultures, peoples, and lands, but I did not have the funds.

An obvious option was to join one of the airlines. The career of air hostess held considerable prestige in those days, but I needed a second language to be considered for that role. A year in Spain gave me the fluent Spanish I needed.

Returning to the UK, I added a three-month intensive keyboard course to my skills, and then took a post as a bi-lingual secretary while I started to look for that air hostess post.

On a personal level, many of my old friends had married or moved away. I needed to build a new social life, but where?

The local library had a list of social clubs, and one with the words 'Travel Club' in its name sounded interesting. I arranged to join a meeting, only to find that the members were all pensioners. I had several other hiccups along the road, but my persistence paid off. Some friends of my parents suggested a local sports and social club. I rang up, and my future husband, Peter, answered the phone. So, I never became an air hostess, but these days I pay my own way to travel around the world.

Portfolio of Experiences

A pattern was emerging. I accumulated a diverse range of work experiences, especially through short assignments. I would take the place of someone on holiday or sick leave, slipping into their role. This was a great way to discover how different companies operated, both the good and the bad. I was developing my portfolio career along the lines described by British business guru Charles Handy in his book *The Empty Raincoat*.

I soon discovered the importance of public relations and marketing in all sectors. The need for effective two-way communications and clear understanding between individuals has, over the years, played an increasing role in my development of key strategies for clients.

Near Misses

By this time, I was married to Peter. Summer was approaching. Our sports car was fun to drive, but on the third day of our European tour, when on the plains in Spain, the car's steering failed, and we slid off the road into a cornfield. (What is it with me and cars?)

Thank goodness it happened then. Earlier that day we had come over the Pyrenees Mountains, between France and Spain. If the accident had happened then, we would have slid over the edge, plunging some 500 feet to our deaths. But perhaps we all have several near misses in life. It's best to learn something positive from them going forward, rather than carrying unresolved fears.

Take Calculated Risks

My earlier teachers had really hammered into me the value of life-long learning. A Public Relations and Marketing diploma beckoned. This could be achieved while working full-time, via a three-year course, attending lectures three nights a week.

At the first evening lecture of my final year, when welcoming his students, the marketing tutor rather condescendingly asked, "Who is the pregnant student?" implying I wouldn't complete the course. But I had the last laugh.

The following summer, while still breastfeeding my first child, I sat those final exams, and then went on holiday. Peter returned home before me to discover I had passed; the diploma was mine. There being no mobile phones in those days, via telegram he told me to celebrate at his expense.

I decided to take home a whole Serrano ham smuggled in the car, as at that time the importation of such raw meat was illegal. It was a relatively small risk, and I don't usually knowingly break the law, but it was well worth it. That ham was delicious.

Gaining Broad-Based Experiences

A period working as a recruitment consultant followed,

leading to another learning opportunity in terms of research for a Fellowship of the Recruitment & Employment Confederation.

My chosen topic was The History of Employee Benefits. This opened up the fascinating world of the early philanthropists, especially the Quakers, who were prime movers in the abolition of slavery, promoting equal rights for women and encouraging peace. Quaker entrepreneurs had a high profile in England, establishing key companies such as Lever Brothers, Cadbury and Friends Provident.

They provided revolutionary employee benefits for their staff, including purpose-built villages such as Port Sunlight and Bournville to house their workforce. Another key Quaker establishment is the Johns Hopkins University in Baltimore. Although I am not religious in the conventional sense, I have a lot of empathy with the Quaker philosophy.

During my second pregnancy I set up my own company. What better time to start a new venture, with baby and business growing concurrently? There was plenty of opportunity for developing problem-solving skills.

Then I secured a five-year contract with a Spanish merchant bank and its associated co-ops, acting as their UK delegate. My role involved researching and identifying British firms interested in selling their technical know-how to help set up turnkey factories in Spain. Sectors ranged from medical disposables and hi-fi equipment to frozen vegetables and automotive components. Here was another opportunity to get into numerous companies and their managements, to see what was working and what were non-viable practices.

Never Assume

One project was to find firms at the cutting edge of technology using carbon fibres to strengthen rubber components for a vast range of applications. My scientific background came in useful here. Having researched, I identified five companies who were developing this field in England and were potentially interested in manufacture under licence agreements. In one week, I took my Spanish client into five different English factories, with the management of each one believing they were the most advanced in this area.

They were clearly unaware of the details of what their competition was doing, and they never enquired if we were in touch with other similar companies, nor did they ask us to sign any non-disclosure documents. They just assumed they were the only ones we were talking to.

Was I the only English person in the world that week to have toured five plants, seen how their processes were being developed and experienced how blinkered their managements were regarding current trends in their sector?

Planned Expansion

As my third pregnancy began, it was once again time to take stock. I had been working at home and now looked for an office. Suitable local premises became available, and we moved in. We were expanding, so I started looking for people nearby who wanted work. I offered flexible hours along with sick pay, not just for the employees, but also when their dependent children were sick. A free lunch was provided to all. And during school holidays, I engaged professional nannies to run our own in-house nursery for employees' children. These moves were revolutionary in the 1990s. Soon I had a dozen people helping to build the company.

I was balancing a family life, motherhood and running a business. I wanted our children to grow up with a second language, and someone introduced me to a Spanish nanny. She was a delightful lady, with limited English, extremely kind to our children, although I think she spoiled them. She was with us for seventeen years, as a nanny, housekeeper and much more.

Always Push Yourself – Keep Listening and Learning

Now I needed to gain recognition for my increasing knowledge and expertise. I enrolled in an MBA programme with the Open University, studying in my spare time, while continuing to work full-time. I was determined to gain this qualification before our children went to university.

The Open University insists everyone covers all key disciplines involved in running a business. There's no focussing on the area where you excel. Three years later, there I was collecting my Masters.

While studying, a serendipitous discovery was the book *Maverick* by Ricardo Semler, which, although published in 1993, is still very relevant today. Semler's radical approach to democratic management involves throwing away the rule book while encouraging employees to self-manage. The result is high employee satisfaction and low absenteeism by running a business in a totally opposite way to that of most corporations. *Maverick* is required reading for my team members and I often give a copy to my clients.

About the time I gained my MBA, the British government launched an initiative to help small- and medium-sized businesses use the services of specialist consultants. I applied for accreditation under this programme. Although ours was only a small company with effectively one principal consultant (me), after completing a sample project, I was assessed as just behind key global management consultancies such as McKinseys, Deloittes and PwC.

During this government programme, which ran for a decade, I completed over 70 projects, in many diverse sectors. This provided plenty of opportunity to keep listening and learning, while taking ideas from one sector, and adapting them to the benefit of other fields.

Since that time, I have worked with a wide range of clients, mainly small- and medium-sized companies. By asking questions and listening, I help individuals take more control over their work, encouraging them to decide things for themselves, draw up their own job specifications and participate in job rotation, where feasible.

So, business owners, keep dreaming, double-check rather than assume, and enjoy the benefits of listening and learning. There are lessons in life all the way along the journey. You just need to keep your eyes open.

*Never Stop
Dreaming, Never
Assume*
*Always Keep Listening
and Learning*

Author's Bio

Liza Jones has been helping company owners and
directors with bespoke analyses relevant to their individual
situations, while providing communications, marketing, and
management consultancy services for more than 25 years.
She works closely with business owners who have reached
a crossroads or are looking for a confidential corporate
facilitator. As an advisor to management, she introduces
constructive, creative support, while adding value.

She guides business owners through the possibilities of
mergers, acquisitions, and investments, developing exit
strategies for those who wish to sell their companies or retire.

She preserves their legacy wherever viable, while supplying a wide assortment of effective solutions enabling the owner to get what they need.

A Fellow of the Chartered Institute of Marketing with an MBA, she has been ranked as a Tier Two Management Consultant by the British Government, the highest level for an individual.

A firm believer in treating every member of the team with respect, whatever their position, Liza creates workplaces no one wants to leave.

She ensured her company gained Investor in People status through introducing revolutionary employee benefits and training schemes.

With well over 100 client relationships, extending from a few months to many years, depending on corporate need, and including multi-nationals to micro-businesses, Liza has the experience of helping companies in very many diverse fields, whether business-to-business or business-to-consumer.

In her spare time, she gives lively and entertaining talks, and has raised many thousands of pounds for the UK charity The Air Ambulance. She is also a best-selling author of several non-fiction books.

Liza speaks Spanish, lives in Suffolk, near Cambridge, England, has been married forever to her loving husband, has three children and five grandchildren.

Contact her on:

📞 +44 20 7834 1066

✉ info@abucon.co.uk

🌐 www.abucon.co.uk

🌐 www.lizajones.co.uk

🌐 www.lizajonesspeaker.co.uk

in https://tinyurl.com/yd3stdwa

in https://www.linkedin.com/in/liza-jones-1066/

Think Smarter!
At the Core of All Adversity
Lies Opportunity

Alireza Mansourian

Think Smarter! At the Core of All Adversity Lies Opportunity

Alireza Mansourian

Others: What does your wall art represent?

Me: It's me, overtaking myself!

An inspirational framed picture hangs on the wall behind the table. My mother bought it for me during my teenage years. In the scene, two agile horses raise dust in an attempt to overtake each other. Their strong muscles appear defined, and it is not clear exactly which one leads. If your eyes fall on it, prompting you to ask for its meaning, I will happily describe how this artwork portrays my life story.

I am typically the last to give up, remembering that tireless effort can carve out a path to guaranteed victory. I must simply remain patient and try to move one step ahead of yesterday. Life often presents itself as a full-fledged and dusty match between you and yourself.

Life Is a Game!

In his epic poem Masnavi, Rumi relates that pain accompanies every birth. Adversity accounts for a large portion of the pain experienced throughout a human lifetime. In alignment with this thinking, one may expect a great "birth" upon facing challenges. I struggle to recall even one of the adversities of my life that did not teach me a valuable lesson.

Just a few months after entering college, I experienced a great love crisis. Although this challenge prompted years of depression, it also represented another birth for me. I considered interacting with friends and reading books to be my only cure during this time. Both the book *Trump 101: The Way to Success* and advice from a good friend to change parts of my lifestyle proved the most influential. Guided by a lot of study, effort, and dedication, I changed my approach in relationships and achieved a dynamic lifestyle by exercising and following a healthy diet plan. Coupled with patience, self-healing practices put me on the path to recovery and turned me into a truly elevated and improved version of my past self. I learned from this experience that much of our perceived adversity might be easily avoided. Though they may feel debilitating, some personal adversities provide us with no educational content. They often happen because we simply are not aware of the effective "rules" of life or do not know how to follow them.

Consider life just like a game of strategy. Humans make up the lucky players and must adhere to certain immutable rules. In similar fashion to other games, the rules will not change according to the players' wishes as they seek desired outcomes. This game's victories occur in special places determined by the rules. People who know the rules better not only possess a more accurate attitude, but also find themselves on the path toward great victory if they develop their unique talents with the proper decision. One who defines his or her actions as accurately as possible will likely encounter far fewer adversities. Of course, some of life's challenges remain inherently unavoidable and may even kill the momentum of experienced and veteran players. In these extreme cases, the only way to persevere is to become stronger.

How much stronger?

Rather than measuring strength in a traditional way, we ought to think of another way to achieve. What makes us shine in this game called life and truly enables us to rise above adversity? Thinking smarter!

Smarter Thinking

This school of thought simply implies that there always exists a smarter thought. It essentially invites you to challenge, and potentially change your mind. Discovering a smarter way of thinking requires a well-adjusted attitude, while applying it requires unparalleled courage, the kind of courage described in the book attributed to John F. Kennedy, *Profiles in Courage*.

The practice of smarter thinking evaluates only "thought" to determine the degree of intelligence. Race and DNA play no role in the process, meaning that anyone can achieve similar progress, regardless of any conceptions surrounding traditional intelligence. 37 trillion cells, acting as your soldiers and outnumbering any country's army, listen incessantly to your command, so aim to feel self-confident in your leadership and to think big. Courage and self-confidence are required to achieve this mindset. We do not say "the smartest" because nothing is absolute in nature and everything is relative. This smart thought mentality considers improving the thinking process to be the only way forward along the path of becoming the best. Perhaps, then, the only downside involves being compelled to think about something at least twice.

The smarter, and therefore stronger, thought must be more successful and permanent in its nature. One might practice the cultivation of such thoughts by reading history and applying some reverse engineering. Understanding the thinking strategy behind the great victories of history proves useful because their strength and permanence remain apparent after all this time. Evaluating them will direct you toward a consistent pattern, both highly accurate and well-defined. Implementing this pattern works the same way as following the principles of the school of thinking smarter.

For instance, the name Satoshi Nakamoto[7] has occupied many minds in recent years. People would like to know what his goal was and why he preferred anonymity to the benefits of being famous. (I hope you can guess the reason after finishing my chapter. Be creative!)

7   The anonymous creator of Bitcoin who has a net worth of billions of dollars.

- Attitude:

Throughout history, especially in the distant past, a select man excelling in intelligence and strength took over the governance affairs for a tribe. Imagine how 2500 years ago, such a position could turn its holder rebellious, while greed to take over neighboring lands could make him a guillotine. The Persian conqueror Cyrus the Great (c. 600-530 BCE) engraved his humanitarian thoughts on a clay cylinder,[8] detailing a strategy with no precedent in the past. At that time, the smart and ambitious kings attempted to overtake one another and become emperors by way of genocide, and often barely conquered no more than a river. These leaders did not recognize the presence of a smarter, and much less violent, solution that would allow an empire to gain control over the regions between the seas in complete peace. Unlike the kings of small lands, Cyrus the Great believed that possession of a great and honorable people ultimately represented a great kingdom. When I consider powerful stories like that of Cyrus, I recall that there is always a smarter thought, so big that small realms cannot grasp it.

If you are among the greatest businessmen in your city, think smarter and make your city bigger. If you want to be a great leader in your field, do not let your field be full of small colleagues. If you are the most successful person in the

---

8   The Cyrus Cylinder is the first bill of human rights. The Cyrus style of governing, based on this cylinder, inspired The Founding Fathers to establish the United States 2300 years later.

family, do not let your family be otherwise devoid of successful people. Help everyone get better so you can improve together and on a larger scale. If you succeed in becoming the best, be proud that your territory is much larger than that of small kings and enjoy the conquests that come in peace. If at first you do not find success, continue believing that living in a large territory brings more prosperity and insures you against adversity. Finally, if you encounter a person who is jealous and afraid to help, tell him or her on my behalf to "think smarter!"

• Decision-making:

You may be surprised to know that the world's largest importer is also the country with the highest gross domestic product (GDP). There, in the United States, the income of one of the smallest states equals the total income of my home country Iran. Those who ruled the American nation could have avoided such a situation, prioritized self-sufficiency, and considered any decision to increase imports on a large scale to be a conspiracy. This choice certainly seems smart and would define the country's reputation as a major creditor instead of a full-fledged debtor. However, as you know, a smarter decision generally exists, and the U.S. leaders chose wisely. The dynamism of the American economy equipped the country with an invisible "gun" that owes much of its power to the placement of the country atop the list of importers. This metaphorical gun comes with an infinite shooting range, does not shed blood directly, and most importantly, can be held only by one player. Within the realm of politics, this gun bears a name: Economic sanctions.

Meanwhile, in business, many consider it a smart decision to pursue one's own profit above all else. Here, the smarter thought is deciding to make as much profit as possible for the other party in any win-win contract. In this situation, your partners fear losing you, thereby jeopardizing their profits, because you have the power to cut off all or part of them without breaking the contract. Meanwhile your customers become addicted to your services. Therefore, while attracting more applicants for both businesses, you simultaneously take the top position of power. Now it behooves any partners to keep you satisfied. Smart people are often good at writing contracts that are only ostensibly win-win. Again, if you witness one of them doing so, feel empowered to tell him or her on my behalf to "think smarter!"

- Giant Goals:

"We choose to go to the moon [three times] in this decade and do the other things, not because they are easy, but because they are hard, because that goal will serve to organize and measure the best of our energies and skills..."

These words belong to John F. Kennedy's speech given at Rice University in 1962. He announced the mandate of landing a man on the moon to Congress before the speech, while his country had not yet sent a single man into space. The dimensions of this goal measured so giant that for many, it could only be achieved in the event of a huge explosion of creativity and technology. In 1969, when Neil Armstrong planted the first human foot on the moon, he sent the following message to the world:

"That's one small step for a man, one giant leap for mankind."

The moon shone no longer in the distance, but rather under human feet. Perhaps no other goal in contemporary history has transformed human life so much. The technology needed to achieve this feat was so vast that it generated a great leap in all sciences, and the moon landing's success became the pride of every human being.

Giant goals, while seemingly costly and dangerous at first glance, have far-reaching consequences. These once-in-a-lifetime moments are born of attitude and decision-making based on smarter thinking. The aerospace, automotive, and peaceful nuclear power industries cost billions of dollars, but they can revolutionize all of science due to the space they take up within a society. Success in these industries requires input from numerous business sectors of a country and inevitably causes a great revolution in fields from clothing and medicine to artificial intelligence and quantum physics! That is why if you find a country in one of the leading industries, you should know that it is homogeneously advanced in all sciences. I suggest that from now on, upon hearing the name Italy, think of all it took to develop Lamborghini besides simply imagining the beautiful city of Venice!

Re-evaluate your goals with smarter thinking. Changing them into giant goals can result from two or more evaluations. Note that the "giant" nature of these goals should not be confused with any notion of inaccessibility. They simply involve a greater amount of energy and skill to accomplish. Giant goals are logically distant and achievable at the same time; just think smarter to achieve them! In other words, challenge your thoughts frequently and on larger scales of time and place.

For example, suppose that you are a student in a non-developed country. Going to Harvard University would be a giant goal for you. This goal can force you to write articles and books, to challenge your knowledge in math and computer science, and to strengthen your English in a short period of time. Moreover, you can be creative and even go beyond thinking smarter! For instance, do not aim for a Harvard lifestyle without integrating fitness and exercise. In this way, you extract additional bene-fits from this goal

No matter how uncomfortable you feel pursuing something at the outset, find importance in how little you resemble your past self after a few years. This transformative sort of proj-ect bears similarity to the Apollo 11 mission in many ways. When you take your first step into a reputable university, you can personalize and articulate that beautiful quote of Armstrong. This is not the end of your work. The processes of immigration, study, and adaptation to the destination country can also be the next giant goals. Truthfully, reaching for your giant goals will usher you into the virtuous cycle. This means that by targeting just one of them, the rest will also show up, bringing about revolutions in all your dimensions and making you a stronger person in the face of adversity. These consecutive benefits arise simply because you have thought smarter once in your life. Define the giant goals of your life: one that you are willing to accept, one that you are unwilling to postpone, one that you intend to win, and the others, too.

Accomplishing the Apollo 11 giant goal made NASA a transnational symbol for science and technology. In fact, the aims of the concurrent Soviet government, including sending the first satellite and man into space, led John F. Kennedy toward that space exploration endeavor. The space rivalry between the United States and the Soviet Union presents perhaps the best example of knowing that if your opponent behaves smarter, it will act in your favor and drive your advancement. Therefore, if each individual human and, consequently, all nations think smarter, the world evolves tenfold. Essentially, thinking smarter is the single most effective action that may lead to Nash equilibrium[9] if people apply it in personal life, business, or even politics.

In an interview, Anousheh Ansari[10] said that rising above adversity becomes possible through the cooperation of human beings with each other and introduced politics as

9   A decision-making theorem within game theory
10   XPRIZE CEO and the first self-funded woman space tourist

the biggest obstacle to achieving this goal. What is referred to in this text as "thinking smarter" leads to extreme human cooperation. Solidarity and utilizing the enormous dimensions of the world are the two principles in which this school of thought comes true. Therefore, true and lasting victory depends on the development of all human beings. The whole point of smarter thinking revolves around the idea of winning a game not by what players choose from the given options, but by something that does not exist in the options at all. They just have to be made and turned into what they should be like diamonds with a lot of polishing. Throughout history, good has always triumphed over evil. This is not a magical process. Rather, doing well is fundamentally smarter and therefore stronger. Those who think smarter choose to be good to put themselves on the path to victory, prestige, and rising above adversity.

In so many great victories of history, one can find a trace of thinking smarter — from those settled in Shahr-e Sukhteh[11] who chose persisting as their giant goal to the Ilam[12] country and modern civilizations. These groups of humans reached a different decision with immense dimensions of thought, a smarter decision! Maybe this world possesses a smarter thought, too; God knows!

---

11   A civilization of several thousand years ago in Iran. The first cosmetic surgery and animation production in history were performed in Shahr-e Sukhte.
12   A country related to 3200 BC on the plateau of Iran. This country is considered the primary cornerstone of the formation of ancient Iran.

It's all about creating. With creativity, one can make the world a brighter place. I ask God to give me the honor of lighting a candle in his world. Now that I am immersed in the dream of realizing my ideas for the future, I like to think of Michael Jackson in Motown 25. He did the moonwalk, on the earth! His goal was to raise standards; for yesterday, today, forever!

Think Smarter!
At the Core of All
Adversity Lies
Opportunity

Author's Bio

When **Alireza Mansourian** was a teenager and should have spent his time in high school, a professor at the Amirkabir University of Technology told him while evaluating his project that it would be better at this age to "play games" instead of inventing. In the same year, Alireza sent six projects in various scientific fields to the Kharazmi Youth Festival, most of which reached higher levels. However, he believes that the professor was right and that if he had spent his time "playing games" at school instead of researching at the university, he would have faced fewer avoidable adversities in life. He considers Thinking Smarter as the always-winning strategy of all "games."

One better step is the story that Alireza repeats every day. He considers self-investment infinitely profitable. In his view, the cheap tutorials that are now available thanks to the internet are like a bundle of $100 bills waiting for their owner. Alireza strengthens himself with a strong love of continuous learning and believes that not a single opportunity should be missed. At the core of all adversity, he's just looking for opportunity. Alireza considered the COVID crisis the best opportunity to invest more. Land and property in the north of Iran, the stock exchange of Iran, and cryptocurrency were the markets of his interest during this period, all of which broke historical records in terms of profitability during the pandemic. By rising above adversity, he has succeeded in increasing his capital by 100 times.

Alireza Mansourian was born in Ilam in 1997 and is a top graduate of exceptional talent schools. He is one of the few engineering graduates who has successfully completed his internship at the IR-T1 Tokamak advanced reactor, researching clean and peaceful energy. Relying on his computer knowledge, he is currently working in the field of investment and management and aspires to expand his non-governmental organization's humanitarian aid. His supermodern NGO named MaNgo is built on Block-chain foundation. Alireza creatively manages it with

Ethereum smart contracts. He is a co-author of *Covid Acts of Kindness* and GUINNESS WORLD RECORD participant of "Most Authors Signing the Same Book Simultaneously".

- www.MansNotes.com
- Alireza@mansnotes.com
- Ma-Ngo.org
- peepeth.com/MaNgo
- twitter.com/orgMaNgo

Following My Heart's Leadings
Finding the Way to My Truth

Mehdi Mazloumi Sani

Following My Heart's Leadings
Finding the Way to My Truth

Mehdi Mazloumi Sani

Having Faith in Myself to Start the Journey

Since childhood, I have always created things in my mind.

When I earned my bachelor's degree and graduated from university, I started to work as a technical engineer in a company that represented a well-known foreign brand in the petrochemical industry's electronic equipment. Less than two months later, the technical representative of that brand came to Iran to visit and monitor our work. The representative and I were together for two weeks, and we visited several cities.

One day, the CEO told me the representative had chosen me to go to England and take a technical course. In the eyes of the other employees, I had been given a great offer and a good opportunity. But I did not feel satisfied with it and could not go along with his offer. Something was telling me that I could design and build my own product.

I was obsessed for two days, mulling over all the plans I had under consideration. What did I really want? Which path should I choose? I decided to consult my heart, where my wishes reside, to see what path really gave me the most peace.

The choice I made was to become a product designer and manufacturer rather than a consumer. This was a fateful and challenging choice, but I had faith in myself. I chose what seemed to be the harder path, but it was the way that was in line with my life's purpose and my larger dreams.

I resigned from that company and designed and built my first product in less than two years.

Knowledge and Skill Acquisition to Create and Leave an Impact

Having parents who were teachers, it has always been a family value to earn high marks in school and receive a decent education. Thus, I set myself the same goal as a child. At university, I majored in electrical engineering (telecommunications) after studying mathematics in high school. I received my master's degree from Tehran Polytechnic University.

From the beginning, I entertained great dreams and wanted to have impressive achievements. I love my field of study, and I thought the world was awaiting my graduation when I was a student. After graduation, I entered the job market, seeking experience and achievement. I had only one thing foremost in mind, and that was learning. I wanted to know how to turn the knowledge I had gained in university into a product. From the first day I began working, I dedicated myself to learning and designing in order to realize what I envisioned. Since I loved my job and enjoyed my achievements, I worked tirelessly, day and night, and it was fun to see the results. Due to my professionalism and perseverance, I have become the project manager or group leader of every company or project with which I worked.

Providing the Best Customer Service: a Choice and a Mission

Ever since I was a student, owning my own technical and engineering company and designing and manufacturing electronic products have been my dreams. In the third year after my graduation, at the age of twenty-five, my friends and I established our first company. Unfortunately, due to a lack of administrative experience, skills, and no sense of unity, the partnership failed, and we dissolved the company.

This was a particularly hard time for me, because with all the ideas, aspirations, and efforts I had contributed around the clock, I did not get the results I anticipated. So, I thoughtfully examined the reasons for my failure and took new steps, with the hope of acquiring new skills.

After years of immersion in research and design, gaining scientific and practical experience, leaving influence in several industrial and national projects, and after a long time spent thinking and challenging myself, I came to the conclusion I should establish my own company. Again, an inner feeling told me I could succeed at this venture. In spite of all my fears, I took the first step to make my dream come true, founding Zinotech to design industrial and telecommunication systems. I defined the company's mission to provide the supply, design, and localization of industrial systems needed by the country, along with the provision of technical knowledge and great customer service.

It did not take long for me to bring together a team of top engineers to provide professional services, including the design of boards, high-tech telecommunications systems, and industrial systems. We proved to our customers and our competition that many products and innovations could be created in the simplest way with the proper expertise and skill.

Since Zinotech is an R&D-oriented company, we are faced with technical and technological challenges every day, and the technical team solves those challenges day and night. One goal keeps everyone hopeful: to provide the best service and support to our customers. Since the production of technical knowledge and an excellent product always have a customer, I determined the company's next steps would be to expand the scope of our products and export to other countries.

It Is Never Too Late to Make a New Choice

One day, in the bustle of technical and engineering work, a friend, who I later had the honor of marrying, invited me to an introductory session on self-knowledge. Despite all my pessimism about psychology, an inner curiosity led me to sign up for the introduction.

In this first session, the course coach asked me to write and submit my biography. Later, when he returned my manuscript, he had written many comments for me, but one sentence always stood out in my mind and started me on my new path. I wrote, "I always have to decide and choose for myself," and the coach wrote to me above that sentence, "Who is this sentence from, based on how you are living your life?"

The coach's comment was a question that has been on my mind ever since. At first, I did not understand the meaning of the comment, and I was in a constantly wavering process of denial and acceptance of it. I wanted to solve it like a mathematical equation. It kept my riveted attention until, over time and by taking more coaching, the meaning of that sentence became clear to me. Since then, I have made great efforts to fully understand it and integrate the benefits of that self-inquiry.

Understanding who I really was and what choices were truly self-directed became my obsession. I wanted to know in how much of my life I was being my true self, and how many beliefs and precepts I had internalized from the significant others who raised me as a child. I struggled to know how much of what I wanted to be had been realized and how much was, in fact, the result of the external forces of my environment. Was my identity then my natural choice, or theirs, or was it both?

I spent a lot of time alone contemplating why, or indeed if, I should limit myself to one field of study, which is all about logic and math, not people, communication, and emotions. One day, I clearly saw the truth and realized how I could live for myself and for the brave new world I wanted to imagine into existence. I decided to answer these important questions and apply what I learned to my life going forward.

Contrary to my belief that I should study a subject and work on it for the rest of my life, I made up my mind to become a student again and start learning, finding answers to all my questions, and unveiling my life's deeper meaning.

Firstly, I learned that the best guide for me is to ask the correct questions. What am I in this world to do? What impact do I want to have on the world? Is there anything in this world to value other than the mathematical logic I learned as a child?

My coaches became my role models and the symbols of my possible abilities. That is why I determined that it is never too late to understand and be truer to myself. At any time and at any age, I can make new choices and create what I want.

Growth Begins from Within

I have consistently been teaching self-knowledge for approximately eight years now. I get help from the best coaches and therapists to rid myself of my own limiting beliefs and obstacles, because I have found that the way to growth and prosperity opens to me when I am free from inner blockages. After I break those restraints, I am no longer my old

Mehdi. Enthusiasm is kindled in me for another breakthrough and to expand the world inside and outside of myself. After overcoming any obstacle, I get a sense of inner satisfaction and empowerment, and I experience extraordinary moments. It is then that I realize that patience and perseverance bring substantial rewards when I have a goal and a choice as my guides.

Fostering a new vision, I choose another bigger goal, which I may be afraid of at first and think I cannot achieve. But then an inner knowing tells me I will achieve this newly chosen goal, just like I have the previous ones. I work by facing fear and using every challenge as an opportunity for problem-solving and breaking of restraints. Nonetheless, resolving some of the challenges may take a long time.

Since studying and university education are important to me, I became a university student again, but this time I got a master's degree in the field of industrial and organizational psychology. Becoming a loving, professional, and effective coach requires long-term planning, training, and skills. During the last eight years, I set long-term goals and made thoughtful plans. I passed specialized courses in addition to those of my original professional occupation. I attended various psychology courses and skills workshops, such as Cognitive Behavior Therapy (CBT), Myers Briggs Type Indicator (MBTI), Intensive Short-Term Dynamic Psychotherapy (ISTDP), Life Skills, and International Coaching.

The Beacon of My Life's Journey

I have defined a new mission for myself in the world: to serve and help people, removing sadness and putting a smile on people's faces, and being a guide and opportunity for others. According to one of my coaches, the world does not need successful people so much as it needs loving ones.

In the previous three years, while I focused intently on what has been described here in this chapter, I learned a lot from COVID-19, as the global pandemic raged across the world. At a time when each of us was looking for success and a means to gain wealth, the world suddenly stood still. Now it seems the only thing that can stop the spread of this disease is the unity, support, and empathy of all human beings, which are qualities the world currently lacks.

Experience has taught me it is never too late to grow and make new choices, and you can do so at any age, regardless of how old you are, so long as you feel content with those choices. Each time I committed to my chosen goal and desire, I experienced this feeling of contentment.

Giving up learning is like giving up on life, so study, growth, and awareness are part of my existential meaning, and I serve myself and others through gaining new understanding. The level of self-care and personal growth I devote to myself is mirrored in my service to others.

Just as aspirations and goals, hopes and actions are essential in life. The same is true about overcoming fear and facing it head-on. The difference between someone who acts and achieves and someone who only dreams is this ability to look fear in the face. If my goal is genuine and inseparable from me, then the world will stand by me to achieve it. People take me seriously to the extent I take my own dream seriously.

The greater good lies in the service and benefit of the collective and the group and the use of our potentials to empower others and do good in the world. Whenever we make someone happy and remove sorrow from someone's heart, we enhance a part of our own being and grow closer to our human essence.

One of the most effective lessons I have learned is from my life coach.

«Service» is the last stage of human development. The path of growth is from mere taking in childhood to pure self-sacrifice in adulthood. Some give as if they have not given and are still trapped in their «I,» but in growth, there is not just «I» but the reciprocity is between «I,» and «we.»

And this "we" is the focus of my life, to share my life experiences and perceptions with others, to bring light to people's hearts and be a patient companion, to cross inner barriers and achieve the shining potential of "we."

Following My
Heart's Leadings
Finding the Way to
My Truth

Author's Bio

Mehdi Mazloumi Sani has a master's degree in Telecommunications Engineering, with more than seventeen years of brilliant experience in R&D and design of electronic and telecommunication products. He has completed more than ten major projects and three national projects. He is a researcher and instructor of courses on the design of high-frequency compact circuits and processing boards.

He is also the founder of ZINOTECH, which provides consulting and R&D services to its clients in the field of telecommunication and electronic technology projects, including the design and manufacture of audio and video transmission equipment. 4G, 5G mobile, and industrial equipment.

Mehdi also holds a master's degree in Industrial and Organizational Psychology and is a student of the International Coaching School under the supervision of the ICF. He has more than eight years of experience in research, learning, and activities in the field of psychology.

Given his background in industry and knowledge of psychology, he also provides organizational advice. Mehdi works closely with his customers and offers relationship management, organizational development and growth, increasing organizational productivity, and organizational diagnostics. He also provides services to his clients using Virtual Reality technology for therapeutic purposes such as reducing job stress, etc.

He holds a CBT certificate, is an ISTDP student, and provides clinical services to his clients as a psychotherapist.

Ways to contact Mehdi:

- www.mehdimazloumisani.com
- www.Zinotech-co.com
- mmazloomi@hotmail.com

Transform Your Life with Education and Study

Growth from Within Holds the Key

Mahmoud Namdar

Transform Your Life with Education and Study
Growth from Within Holds the Key

Mahmoud Namdar

Education and Military Service

When I finished high school in 2000, I was not accepted into university. At that time, I thought success meant getting accepted into a university, and the only way to succeed was to obtain a university degree. I was in a terrible mental state and thought my life was ruined. I was under a lot of pressure from all sides, especially from my family members.

After three months, I joined the army, which became one of the best times of my life, allowing me to gain a lot of experience and appreciate what I had. Military service lasted two years, after which I started working as a goldsmith.

The Gold Business Period

Our family's enterprise was the gold business. I could not select a different future career, because that decision was my family's choice.

However, I was unsatisfied and disliked the work, which caused me a lot of turmoil. Nonetheless, I almost accepted that it would be my entire life's work. I considered the job to

133

be an old man's career role, because it required no effort or creativity and did not lead to personal growth. I thought to myself, "Does this mean my life has been reduced to a twenty-meter shop? Is that all there is to life?"

Mine was a daily routine without opportunities for growth. I had always wanted to have a challenging job and to grow every day. In my resolved state of being, all I did was go to the store in the morning, put in my day's work, and stay home at night. I felt like a moving corpse whose life was being sucked out from within.

While it is true that I had a fair income, among the wealthiest in the city, mine wasn't a job I was happy with, and the affluence did not impress me. I felt I deserved more and needed to take action, but I didn't know how or what to do. I continued in this miserable role until 2008, when my shop was burglarized one night, and all my property was destroyed. Assuredly, I was not in a good situation, and I had no idea what to do or what I wanted going forward.

Relying on a gracious God, I had to start over from the ground up. Because I was always hopeful about the future and considered myself to be a hard-working and persistent person, I did not give up. Because I liked working in a group, I closed the gold shop, and left to start a new career.

Establishing an Automotive Dealership Business (Iran Khodro Agency)

A new path in life was opening to me, such a wonderful experience. As the saying goes, I entered the land of the unknown to establish my own sales agency, selling Iran Khodro's cars in Zarrin Dasht City, one of the southernmost cities in Fars Province.

I had no background knowledge or business plan for this step and started working experimentally with about thirty people. I remember that I was afraid of speaking to my staff on the first day of work. It would be an understatement to say that my knowledge and agency training were lacking. We threw all our challenges back to the parent company and its employees because we were not able to take responsibility.

Our dealership was an extremely weak representative of the car company because of these issues. In fact, we went through a downward trend for four years, a result of our moment-by-moment choices. We thought people should come to us and buy cars from us, and our sales were low. The root problem and the way to fix it were unclear to my staff and to me.

This lack of understanding was slowly destroying my career trajectory and my life. I was angry about the downward spiral, and I felt very upset with myself. I used to hold daily meetings in the agency in an attempt to improve our success. On several occasions, I sent my staff to neighboring agencies for training.

The other agencies responded uncooperatively because we were their competitors.

I had invested all my assets in this business. Its sales results were so poor I had no money to pay salaries and living expenses. My mental state was very bad, and my thoughts were increasingly negative. It bothered me so much that I was having a dreary and routine life again. Because I did not know what I wanted, and I had not learned important lessons from my past job, I was repeating the same kind of life while working in a new position. Criticism, especially from my family members, added to the other issues.

At any given moment, we made business decisions based on trial and error, and most of them proved wrong. Ours was one of the weakest dealerships. We believed that problems would be solved on their own, over time, and with experience. This lackluster trend continued until September 2017.

Education Paves the Way to Growth and Transformation

My work force evaporated that year because I failed to pay their salaries. There were times when unpaid people came to my door at night to collect the money owed them. Ultimately, we were left with only three agency employees, and no customers came to us. The agency had become as deserted as an empty football field, and days passed without any improvement in that trend. I was apprehensive and often terrified. Nonetheless, I have always had hope for the future, and I persevered, believing that unseen help was coming.

In the same year, Iran Khodro Company decided to hold management and human resources classes for its top agencies in Tehran. In a letter, the company asked interested agencies to participate. Fars province had ten agencies, none of which welcomed the idea of participation in the classes. I was looking for a way out of my precarious situation, so I decided to attend these classes to pass the time.

Every human being has a turning point in life. Prior to registering for the series of classes, I was not interested in learning or studying.

The first-class meeting was held at the Industrial Management Organization in Tehran, Iran's capital. The topic was *human resources*, and it was taught by Mr. Mehrdad Hashemi. Within twenty minutes after class began, I was fully focused on the material, and a profound shift occurred in my thinking. I "drank" in the subject matter like a thirsty person. As the class progressed, I absorbed everything we discussed, getting more eager to learn, just like a lover who has found his beloved.

My hope increased, and I felt positive about myself. Having a happy disposition motivated me to work and to live life more fully. I realized that my life and career path had to change 180 degrees. This realization made me extremely happy. It promised me a new beginning, and sparks of change flashed through my mind. I gained a greater sense of motivation, happiness, and communication in every area of my life.

These classes were held once every two weeks in Tehran. By participating in them, which was one of the best times of my life, I gradually became interested in education and study. And as a result, I was thankful to God. I still am.

In addition to the classes held on Fridays, I started leading classes for my agency staff on Mondays to help them evolve and progress as a team. In the beginning, I was called delusional and told I was out of my mind by the staff members. In the end, they began to undergo a similar change to mine, and we started 2018 with only a little training. We conducted an incomplete goal setting exercise for the first time, but the staff members' mindset had changed. To all of us, it became apparent that everything we hoped to achieve was created first in our minds, and we should make the changes that would bring about new results.

My employees started working with double the energy they had before, and in the same year, we sold an amount equal to five years' sales, because their belief in themselves had changed. As a result, our income increased, and our enthusiasm and hope returned. Life was getting sweeter for me, and I was thankful to God.

From that year on, I made studying and learning a major priority in my life and work. I continued with great masters such as Dr. Alireza Azmandian, Dr. Shahab Anari, Dr. Alireza Shiri, Saeed Mohammadi, and Professor Omrai to seek to know myself and find myself, because human growth begins with self-knowledge.

The Prophet of Islam says, "He who knows himself knows the Lord."

Also, a Persian poet says,

There is no world outside of you, all in yourself.

Seek within, for the world is in yourself.

By setting these words to be the motto of my life, I made teaching and learning my top priority.

My daily life and work became happier as a result, and I had a sense of inner satisfaction.

In fact, this growth in my profession and work resulted in me becoming interested in the education industry, pursuing my philosophy of life, and discovering my mission. Because of this, I now read books every day, whereas I did not believe in reading and the benefits of learning before 2017.

Since that time, I've read books like Darren Hardy's *The Compound Effect* and Napoleon Hill's *Think and Get Rich*, which changed my mindset. I realized the only way to succeed in any field is to study and acquire knowledge, and I was a rich and happy person because of this experience.

Now, I have great aspirations and a desire to excel internationally. I am currently building another company and setting up an educational institution to serve my compatriots. Throughout my life, everything has revolved around me, and I am my most valuable possession. The more I invest in myself, the more successful I become. An individual, a business, or even a country can only develop and grow if they study and learn. The first step to change external circumstances is for humans to change themselves. The outside world will also change when I change. There is an old saying that states: *What is in the jar is what pours out.*

As I look back on my life today, I am reminded of Steve Jobs's 2005 lecture at Stanford University, where he said that, "When you connect the events of your life, you realize that everything in life works for your benefit, and the universe works for you in every way."

I always try to feel good and not regret the past. Having a positive attitude and never giving up is the first lesson we need to learn. All things work in our favor in life, and whenever anything happens, it leads in the direction of our growth and development. There are lessons to be learned from this. We will be able to enjoy our lives to the fullest if we keep a positive perspective on life events and know that difficulties and issues make us stronger.

Second, all problems in this world can be solved by learning, and if we make education the main tool of our work, our growth rate will be extremely high.

The third lesson is that human beings definitely will find their way if they persevere in their work. Perseverance keeps us from giving up. Having strong inner motivation, I never gave up and always believed that I would either succeed or would create a way.

The fourth lesson is that the main capital of any economic enterprise or country is its human resources. Any job will be improved if we train our staff, develop them, and improve them individually, because by improving their character, our business will also grow.

The fifth lesson is to do whatever you love. We are often led astray in discovering our mission by the money we hope to earn. We should try to discover our interests over time and move along this path to have a happy life.

The sixth lesson is that becoming a gem is a very long and difficult process. We must try to choose very very big goals and work toward them in very, very small steps.

Transform Your Life with Education and Study
Growth from Within Holds the Key

Author's Bio

Mahmoud Namdar has been the manager

of two Iran Khodro and Saipa sales agencies for eight years and has succeeded in obtaining the top rank in the country for four consecutive years. He has 60 staff members who can provide you with new cars and help you invest in the car industry. He has been teaching for five years and has trained 1,000 people to date. He specializes in personal growth and development and business growth. He is a member of the NLP and Coaching Association of Iran and has a coaching and NLP certificate from the European ECA.

🌐 www.1dar100.com

✉ mahmoudnamdar68@gmail.com.

Crossing the Mind Bravely
Taking Risks to Succeed

Mobin Nassaj

Crossing the Mind Bravely
Taking Risks to Succeed

Mobin Nassaj

He[13]

After dinner, when I went to my bedroom to rest, I saw a letter on the table with my name written on it.

I opened the letter and read it carefully and realized that it was from *him*.

It had been a few weeks since I had heard from *him*, and I almost forgot about *him*. I did not want to remember *him* again after all I had done to forget *him*.

He did something for me; because *he* is always on the prowl, I can bravely ignore his words and go on.

---

13   He is the thoughts, worries, barriers to action, deterrent beliefs, etc., who when we want to go beyond our safe boundaries and try new things, makes us nervous and afraid to do so. In other words, when we get used to a certain lifestyle, our mind does not want to accept new or alternative habits, thus dissuading us from using them.

All we have to do is ignore those feelings once and for all and take that risk and step out of our comfort zone so that we can grow and prosper and change our lives forever.

COVID-19

Maybe this isn't the right time[14]. Wouldn't it be better to wait until this virus is gone before starting?

This situation will definitely lead to failure for me.

But it may take a few years for the situation to return to normal.

Currently, I cannot think of a worse time to start. What crazy person starts a business in this situation? Why on earth do I want to do this now?

I still have time, and I can enjoy the quarantine for now.

What stupid thoughts come to my mind, really! In the worst situation that the world has ever seen, what ideas do I entertain!

Instead of obsessing about these things, it would be better to entertain myself with movies, series, the Internet, etc., so I can forget about them and stop making myself miserable.

People generally believe that starting a business now, during a pandemic, is a bad idea, and they have to wait until the situation returns to normal. This is a situation in which it is not yet known when things will return to normal. Another year? Another ten years? Perhaps never!

---

14   Research by the University of Manhattan shows that entrepreneurs became 30% more creative during the pandemic.

You should not wait for the *right* circumstances to appear. These circumstances may never exist or could only be created by us. And, in fact, it is only we who can create them.

Don't give up on yourself because of the situation, and get to work. No one has ever been given a chance to succeed without working for it. Let's put this mindset aside and not question a successful person's efforts.

The least you can do to begin and succeed in COVID-19 times is to invest time and effort in your personal development. Read as many books as possible and make it a good habit, because books provide strength and courage to think like a successful person.

Your creativity will diminish day by day if you don't read books, and you won't have any more wealth-creating ideas.

Attend courses taught by successful people, learn from their years of experience, and apply that knowledge. There is no magic formula for success, but this new learning can serve as a roadmap for you. It may also provide shortcuts that will prevent you from repeating the mistakes the successful people made and help you achieve your goals faster.

Fear of *Him*

Whenever I want to do something meaningful, *he* shows up, and *he* distracts me. It looks like *he* doesn't want me to do anything, but enough is enough!

I do not want to listen to *him* this time.

But *he* may be right. I may not be able to do what I'm dreaming of doing successfully.

As always, it makes me hesitant. To whom should I listen now? Myself or *him*?

I know I will succeed if I do this, but what if I do not?

I will lose all my capital investment, and I will have no place to sleep. But if I can make it successful, this forty-meter house and this good-for-nothing car will be gone for good.

Let me ask my wife; maybe she can help me.

"Do you think I should do it tomorrow, or should I let it go?"

"Again? Don't you want to let go of *letting go*?" she said.

"I'm afraid that nothing will go as I expect."

"Nothing turns out the way you hope it will, but it has to be done, because you have been trying for tomorrow for so long," she said.

"What do I do if I go bankrupt again?"

"I know this time will be different. This time, you can do it," she assured me.

"So, wake me up early in the morning."

The closer you get to the deadline, the more fear and anxiety you have.

The risk you are taking can be one of the most important decisions you make in your life, so don't underestimate it. You have been selected for it, and you need to put your best foot forward.

Always remember, and always be thankful, to those who have helped you in this situation. They have been instrumental in your success, and without them, you wouldn't be in this position. So, remember to thank those who have helped you get to where you are now.

Resignation

As of today, I am leaving my ridiculous job so I can devote all my time to my personal business.

If I fail, I will have no job, no house and even my old wrecked car will be gone.

There is no rush. I'll wait until tomorrow. I'll think more about it. Maybe I'll consult some people.

Me: "I want to resign from my job. Can you give me some advice?"

Friends: "Are you crazy? You want to leave this job with all these benefits and go to one in which it is uncertain where you will end up?"

Boss: "If you want to go, leave. But once gone, you will no longer have a place in this company."

Most people do not support you in such instances, because you want to do something they also may have wanted to do one day, or your plans may seem impossible to them. Your actions prove them wrong. This means they were not up to such a task, while it was not impossible. So, they will try to hold you back at the beginning for their own peace of mind.

Your parents, on the other hand, are not upset about your success and do not want to disappoint you. Since they are afraid of seeing your suffering, they do not want to see you fail. Unfortunately, acting on this fear of failure is an entirely wrong approach.

Please do not be influenced by limited mindsets. Do not give in to the wrong judgments of the nay-saying people. Do what is best for you, and do not listen to words that do not give you hope.

Maybe the same people who make fun of you now will one day be proud to have known you, and perhaps they won't. Do not make this your aim.

His Return

What is your obsession with getting rich? Don't you realize that in order to become rich, you have to turn your back on humanity and all moral principles?

Definitely not! This is not what I want to be. I always want to adhere to my own moral principles.

It may be time for me to step aside after all. Why did *he* show up again?

Every time I want to take a big step, I have to cross *him* first. There must be a reason.

What is *his* problem with me?

I know that *he* wants nothing but the best for me, but that keeps me from moving. It's time for me to be reckless. I'm done with *him*.

However, everything is currently going smoothly. I just got used to my new house and car.

Perhaps I should be more cautious.

I do not want to embarrass my son by returning to my previous situation. The circumstance has caused him many hardships, and his friends have always ridiculed him because of it. I don't want to face those problems again. I want to be a good father. I want my son to be proud of me.

Fear of failure and feelings of responsibility are perfectly normal, regardless of the situation. However, one thing you should always remember is not to limit your success because of a fear of failure. As Grant Cardone says in *The 10X Rule:*

"When people start limiting the amount of success they desire, I assure you they will limit what will be required of them in order to achieve success and will fail miserably at doing what it takes to keep it."

Do not run away from failure because of your fear of it. Accept failure as a part of your path to success. Be reckless, enjoy the route, and be prepared for your wheels to be punctured in the middle of the road. But remember that a wheel that is not punctured does not need to be fixed. So do not waste your time thinking about fixing a wheel that is in perfect shape.

Rest

Perhaps now that I am away, everything will get ruined and all I have done be destroyed. Is a week's travel worth all the stress?

It would have been safer for me if I did not go on this trip and dealt with my work conservatively, staying at home.

For a few years, I have not traveled, so perhaps a few days of rest can't hurt.

My business is still not in a state where I can abandon it for a couple of days, even though I know I need this trip. You cannot travel if you are stressed. Is it not better to stay put this year, and travel next year with a mind at peace and a heart ready to enjoy? Maybe not even the next year. It's a bit early. Maybe in two years.

There are times when people become so engrossed in their businesses they forget about their responsibilities regarding their family and friends, and even their health, and do not make time for such important matters.

One of the regrets people have on their death beds is wishing they had more time for recreation and to be with their family. There are many successful people whose children treat them like strangers, because they worked so hard to make life easier for their children. But an easy life is not all the child wants, and most children will not cope well with parents who are often absent.

Resting and having fun will increase your performance in all areas of life, so do not be stingy with the time you devote to fun and vacations. Mind your health, both physical and psychological. There are things other than wealth in your life that are worthy of your focus and attention.

Last Words

In anticipation of writing this chapter, I searched for an inspirational story to begin, but I couldn't think of any. Then I decided to make up my own inspirational tale, one that could be made into an animated version one day. It turns out that I am no pro at this, but if you enjoy it, then I may finish it one day.

My main goal, as I write this, is to encourage you to take initiative and begin. Beginnings always terrify us, but that terror is all in our heads. *He* will always be there, too, helping us come up with all kinds of excuses, making the inevitable happen, and forcing us to let go. After a few years of taking no action, we will find our life the same as it has always been, only with us being a little older.

But it is never too late to start and make a change. All you have to do is to persevere and keep going. When on the road to your success, you will see that everything changes. You will be an entirely different person, and nobody will remember who you used to be.

Successful people say, "Success is not difficult, or, it is difficult but not impossible[15]."

As a last note, I would like to emphasize that money comes to you through serving others and creating value for others. It doesn't matter if you have all the wealth in the world; if you aren't in good spirits, it is of no use to you.

Babak Badkoubeh: "I once had an old car without a license plate, but in that same old car, I was happy, and I would laugh all the time. Likewise, I once had a luxury car, but I sobbed in it. Then I realized it wasn't about the car or the money. It is you who should be in good spirits before possessing all that.

It is better to wash a wedding dress in a tin pan than to wash a mourning dress in a gold pan[16]."

---

15   Although this path begins with a lot of challenges, every month you can compare the obstacles from the previous month to the current one, and you can see that the obstacles were easier to overcome. Throughout this path, this process continues. Eventually, you stop calling those problems *problems*, as in the initial stages they tend to be purely financial and slow down your progress. After you pass this stage, you will encounter problems outside the financial framework.

16   A Persian proverb meaning that it is always better to be happy but poor, rather than sad but rich.

Crossing the Mind Bravely
Taking Risks to Succeed

Author's Bio

Mobin Nassaj is the founder and CEO of
Netketmarket online store. In its first phase, he intends to sell watches through a sales cooperative system. Mobin has chosen watches as the first product of his store because his family has been in this profession for several decades.

He believes that the network marketing and sales cooperative systems in Iran are not very well known. By developing them, he can serve his country. He is also interested in financial markets and is active in the digital currency market. He is right now studying architecture in university.

Mobin believes it isn't always as early as we think. We ought to act as soon as possible before a good opportunity is lost.

📷 netketmarket

✉ netketmarket@gmail.com

✉ nassaj.mobin@gmail.com

🌐 www.netketmarket.com

The Hidden Blessing in Failure

Learning to Go with the Flow

Navid Omidi

The Hidden Blessing in Failure Learning to Go with the Flow

Navid Omidi

First. Algae City

Once upon a time, beneath the blue sky in the heart of a dense forest, there was a roaring river. At first, it was not yet a river but was a spring, coming out from under the rocks, from the heart of the mountain. Slowly, it gathered with other springs. At this point of our story, it became a river, roaring and surging, sometimes calm and sometimes angry and turbulent.

The story of the river may be interesting to you, but I want to take you to the depths of its water, to the bottom of the river. During the years that the river flowed, people built houses and started a life for themselves at the bottom of the river. No one knows where they originally came from, but they have lived there for years. At its bottom, the river was less turbulent and roaring, and all kinds of grasses, algae, and plants grew in the riverbed. The people had been feeding on these for years and living their lives as bottom dwellers.

In this village of our story, Algae City, there had been a law for many years, maybe for centuries:

We cling to the bottom of the river.

The people of Algae City learned from their parents, and they had learned from their parents, that to survive, they had to cling to the bottom, to the algae and weeds. Since these plants had strong roots at the bottom of the river, it was the only refuge from the river's roaring waves. The people also anchored their houses to algae and hardy plants, so the river would not carry them away to some horrible end.

As their children got older and slowly learned right from wrong, this was the first thing they learned, to anchor themselves to the river bottom's algae and plants. Many stories about people who broke the law and had a bit of adventure were told at nightly gatherings. There was the man who had gone untethered, and the stream pounded him on the rocks and cliffs in its path till his skull was crushed. Another had been swallowed by the big fish. Another died of starvation since there were no algae elsewhere in the riverbed! The people of the village had a strange talent for storytelling, and there were countless stories which all had one thing in common: irreversible calamity and death.

Along with these stories there was one other, a legend about a savior. It was said that many years ago the people of Algae City saw a creature in the sky, floating in the heart of the waves. No one knew if this creature was a man, an angel or a spirit. Nonetheless, it was seen clearly and was named *Savior*. I will soon explain why.

The savior swam upstream without being crushed by the rocks and tried to communicate something to our people from a distance. But he could not be heard, nor could his gestures be understood before he disappeared from the sky. The next day, the people who saw the savior thought about their experience, wondering what the savior was and what the savior wanted to say. And the stories started again.

One who was quite a physicist said the savior was born of illusions, and the reflection of sunlight from certain angles could create the image of a human being in the sky. Another said the savior was one of the unlucky ones who broke the law from one of the upstream villages. He let go of the floor and probably went further onto the rocks below and died, so there was a chance he was shouting to ask us for help.

Many people said that the savior was not a human being at all but an angel who wanted to save us. The savior was telling us to get ready for his return, because he wanted to take us with him to those heights where a good city full of blessings would be our new home.

Since this sighting, the name of our friend became the savior, and the legend of a savior has been narrated in various forms at night gatherings for many years.

Second. Savior

For many of its residents, that day was like all the days of God. But for one, something was different, like a flipped switch, a decision, a change.

He had lived there from birth, had opened his eyes to the people of Algae City and had grown larger day by day. As a child, he was a dreamer. One day he dreamed himself in a quiet city without the raging waves, in a beautiful house. The next day he was on a spaceship that could not be harmed by a wave or a rock, and it was flying high in the sky all by itself.

Growing up and learning to read, the small library of Algae City was his hangout, and his love was fiction, mythical people or creatures, strange lands and distant cities. As he got older, he read *Jonathan Livingston Seagull*, maybe more than ten times. Many nights before going to sleep he imagined himself in the shape of Jonathan who one day walked and stepped on everything he had heard as a child. His peers sometimes stigmatized him because of his fantasies. Though he talked about his dreams when he was younger, he gradually stopped talking. In his silence, he followed his fantasies and dreams.

The common ground of all his dreams was that in none of them was he in Algae City. The cities of his dreams were all quiet, and none of their people were afraid of the raging river.

He spent years with these dreams and eventually reached the age of 39. And on that day, he decided to go, without any words, for words bring logic with them, mathematical logic; and in his inner world, there was no such thing.

Early in the morning, before the river was bathed in sunlight, he packed a bag while out of sight of the others, and before anyone else awoke, he launched himself into the river, along with a mountain of fears, ignorance, and uncertainty.

The waves of the river moved him with all their might, and the only thing he could do was to embrace himself so that he would not be harmed if he hit a rock, or to move his limbs a little to keep himself away from the rocks.

Time passed. His movements were still with the current, and he did not hit any stone, as if by some miracle. He rose higher in the stream and found there was no stone above. The river was bright with the light shining from above, and down below, Algae City had awakened. He didn't even need to concentrate on his movements anymore. It was just roaring water and that was it; he need not fear.

When he had calmed down a bit, he started waving his arms to the people below in Algae City with excitement, shouting to them, "Leave and come with me! Nothing bad will happen to you!"

One or two people who saw him brought the rest and a group of people pointed at him. But no one could hear him. After a while, he could no longer see the city and its people, they were so small, their images receding, and the *savior* left their field of vision too.

His watery journey went on for a few days. He didn't have to do much, just let himself go and the water took him away

THE HIDDEN BLESSING IN FAILURE

with its current. As the river calmed and got bigger, he reached its surface. He learned for the first time where the light was coming from, a sky much bigger and bluer than the sky of his city on the riverbed. He had read about some of the things he now saw in children's fantasy books: the vast blue sky, the birds, the warming rays of the sun.

And he kept going, until one day his dream came into view, the day when the roaring river was no longer just a river. He had reached a vast ocean with a very beautiful shore, and a little beyond that were trees and dense forest. Yes, he had reached a place he had been dreaming of for many years, one he had only seen in the pages of books.

Third. The Hidden Blessing in Failure

Maybe it all started for him from that angry day, when the organization where he had worked for years ignored him. The promotion and position he worked for years to achieve, and sacrificed so much for, now belonged to someone else.

In the weeks that followed, his whole being was filled with anger and frustration in response to this terrible blow. He felt like a boxer in the ring, when hit with a heavy fist. It may have been the heaviest fist of his life, and its impact confused him for a while. Those moments of confusion and excruciating pain, for some, may appear to be superficial, yet something shifts beneath the depths of their warrior existence. There is a kind of inner movement in which the person before and after may be different from head to toe. Confused, the opponent stays with this newborn person and endures the terrible power of the blows, eventually losing.

Navid, after the blow of an organizational fist, was confused and frustrated for months. But it was this fist that shook him into action, to follow his dreams of freedom, liberation, and entrepreneurship, after twenty years of employment. Another promise seemed to be born in him, different from anything he had ever lived before.

He remembered that twenty years before, he had chosen his field of study based on job advertisements. Yes, in those days he saw 40-50 openings for mechanical engineers, 10-15 for electrical engineers and two or three for other categories. He had the potential to be accepted into any field of study he wanted and to do so wherever he wanted. He chose to pursue mechanical engineering when his true love was physics and solving its problems. He quickly became one of the 40-50 people in one of the newspaper job advertisements, and he was in that role for the next twenty years in the aforementioned organization.

Some people find their way in the beginning. For some, it takes two or three years. For others, it takes five, ten, or fifteen; and for a very, very large number of people there is never a chosen and desirable path. For Navid, the time it took was twenty years till he realized the value of his mind, body, will, and existence.

To be more precise, he had always been concerned with the intersection of meaning, employment, and entertainment in a pursuit that belonged to him and not to anyone else. During the past twenty years, he left a lot of his desires to continue his studies in his field, his specialization in the organization and its development abroad. Specifically, his passions for yoga, massage, music, writing, and trading in the financial markets had been neglected. "Clinging to algae on the riverbed" had always prevented him from balancing his personal life with employment. The proverbial "carrots" of his organization were not ineffective either.

Previously, these life issues made him depressed and anxious, but today it seems all these were choices he could have made for his path, to create the meaning he desired. He spent weeks and months meditating deeply to discern which of those hobbies could be his seed for fruitful personal growth.

In those days, he learned from a professor that he should focus exclusively on one goal, one path, one mission. The moment that focal decision is made, he would receive messages from every corner. So, Navid considered his options:

- An international yoga instructor with thousands of students.
- International massager with his own massage therapy academy.
- A successful physicist, researching and working at the best universities in the world.

- A successful novel writer and Nobel Laureate in Literature.
- Specialized engineer of cranes and their standards.
- A successful trader and analyst of international financial markets.

These were all images that he nurtured in those weeks and months so he could make a choice, and what a difficult choice it was! He loved all these options and had traveled a short path in each of them, and that made him feel attached. A person's goals are like his children, and it is not easy to leave any child for another. He had no choice but to choose.

He wrote and wrote for hours, and he talked many times with those around him about his interests, his talents, his happiest and deepest moments. He wanted to see in what role they could imagine him doing better. It was as if he were solving a complex puzzle, the puzzle of the dream image of his years to come, and every day the picture seemed to become clearer.

After a few challenging months of considering all options, he chose to be a trader and financial market analyst. How enjoyable it was for him in the days that followed, the indescribable pleasure of sowing the seeds of his existence and waiting for it to become first a seedling and then a fruit-bearing tree! Waking at night, sacrificing fun, relaxation, and the pleasures of spending time in chosen endeavors; these days were behind him. How incredibly good it was to nurture something in himself! Like a pregnant mother, whose baby grows in her womb all her life, she enjoys many things about the new life growing within her. So it was for Navid.

He completely focused on trading and analysis, sought new training and organized his knowledge of the topic, and nowhere did he introduce himself as a mechanical engineer. He was a trader and a financial market analyst and rode on the waves of charts amidst the multitude of financial instruments. He also started teaching. Learning and teaching were always some of his pleasures, and what better way to teach his specialty! We cannot say that everything went smoothly. He had ups and downs, joys and stresses. Moments of doubt were not few for him, but faith in his goal and the amazing force that always supported him, kept him on track.

And today, years after he made that choice, the Omid Analytical Academy is a growing and fruit-bearing tree. By continuing its professional training activities in the markets, every day is better than the day before. This academy is a platform for the training and growth of all people who find their way in a variety of financial markets.

Navid believes in the hope that one day we can all live the mission of our being.

*The Hidden
Blessing in Failure*
*Learning to Go with
the Flow*

Author's Bio

Navid Omidi is an analyst, trader, and lecturer in international financial markets. His approach to Forex, stock, futures, digital currencies, and all markets with reliable price data, in general, is quite efficient and effective.

Navid is a successful role model for courageous people who decide to change course and start a new business in their middle age.

His childhood dream was to earn money and wealth through analytical and mental activity in a free and open job without time and space restrictions, and today he lives that dream.

In 1995, Navid was ranked 35th out of hundreds of thousands of candidates in the university entrance exam in his country, and then in 2000, he graduated from the best university of technology in his country (Sharif University of Technology) in the field of mechanical engineering. In the following years, he mastered the design principles and standards of overhead cranes and became a national brand in the steel industry, which was his field of work.

In addition to this career, in line with his dreams and long-term interests, he tried and experienced various activities such as writing, photography, music, yoga, and trading in the financial markets, and finally, at the age of 39, he made his big decision to continue and focus on trade in financial markets.

Navid has been active in the financial markets ever since. Continuous learning is one of the principles of his team's and his own work. Teaching has always been one of his greatest pleasures and strengths.

To date, dozens of people have had successful experiences attending his comprehensive training courses, and as a result, they have chosen financial markets as their career and method of earning money and wealth. The strongest class analysts have also started working as colleagues in his analytical team.

The **Omidinvest** educational and analytical academy was founded by him and is a suitable base for financial market enthusiasts.

🌐 www.omidinvest.com

📷 @omid.invest

✈ T.me/omidinvest

✉ Navid.omidi@gmail.com

Why? When? Where?

Rising above Challenge and Adversity

Barbad Raeisi

Why? When? Where?
Rising above Challenge and Adversity
Barbad Raeisi

An accomplished painter was drawing on the paper with a brush.

An ant noticed the brush moving and said to his companions, "That brush makes fabulous drawings on the paper."

A second ant said, "These imprints are works of the illustrator's hand, and the originator of this wonder are the fingers."

A third ant chimed in, "The brush and the movements of the fingers are made by the artist's arm."

A fourth one said, "The movements of the arm are made by the human body."

Every ant reflected a reason, until the wisest of them said, "You have observed the human form, unconscious when asleep and dead; sobeit without his soul and mind, there shall be no portrait. The mind is the origin of the illustration."

But even that ant was unknowing that the mind and the soul are likewise subject to God's will, and if God's grace and compassion were not endowed to the mind, the man would have been immersed in his idiocy. So, the Great Lord is the origin.

--Mawlana, Masnavi Ma'navi

As a child, I suffered from severe stuttering and was unable to speak until the age of three. Various tests and speech therapy sessions enabled me to start uttering words little by little. My stutter persisted until early in my school days. When I could not speak properly and completely, my friends ridiculed me, and this led to feelings of isolation and anthropophobia, a fear of people. The speech therapy sessions hastened my recovery, thanks be to God.

I grew up in a family with not one single member professionally pursuing an art form. Subsequent to my anthropophobia treatment, my brother and I enjoyed watching theater productions, and at times we watched the actors rehearsing. As time went by, I developed an interest in drama, and I contemplated how to step into it. I encountered strong opposition from my family, which came along with various reasons and arguments, including my youth, my stutter, and that a child as young as I was must exclusively study his school lessons. Nonetheless, I was determined and yearned to become an actor. Wishing for something is different from wanting it; wishing is the passive state of wanting.

Eventually, I started doing drama in spite of several challenges. For instance, during school days, we had to rehearse four to five hours and seven to eight hours on holidays, with actors of twice or three times my age. The next challenge was that no one there was my peer. And the most important challenge was my stutter, which, thank God, was almost resolved, except it intensified when I was under great stress. Thanks be to God, I did not disengage and continued to meet the challenges. I enjoyed the course of my acting life.

There is a proverb often heard in our family which states: "Water is very pleasant, but it makes no lovely sound until it collides with an obstacle (big and little rocks)."

Our human lives are just as pleasant as water, yet we do not truly flourish if we face no problem to solve, which is when we may appreciate the precious gem God has endowed within us. If we believe that a moment of happiness and energy is just meant for our destination, we neglect to enjoy the whole road and to be thankful to God every single moment of our journey.

Going back to my story, little by little, I managed to convince my family to have me professionally trained in an acting institute (thank God). At the first session of my trial performance, I faced mocking laughter and was ranked last. One hundred and eighty days later, at the final exam, my performance surprised everyone, and I was ranked first in the institute, thank God. In the summer of the following year, I performed in three dramas and, by the grace of God, good things happened in all three of them. Two years later during the summer, I participated in seven dramas, a noteworthy record for someone of that age. Rehearsing to perform in those seven dramas, I worked from nine in the morning until one the next morning (about fifteen or sixteen hours), sometimes even forgetting to eat. In such cases, I remembered the phrase I used to often hear in my home: "There's a price for everything." Learning is an important principle for successful people, so keep learning all the time.

Once I finished those acting jobs, I wanted to promote myself and enroll in training courses at a higher level. When an advanced French drama professor held a performance workshop in Iran, I was very thankful to God for that opportunity.

Once the workshop came to a close, I was delighted with another miracle of God, the Most Benevolent, the Most Merciful, and was invited to France to receive further training and to eventually do drama there. However, I decided not to go for several reasons, including my youthful age.

I experienced many ups and downs along this path, until I decided to professionally experience drama director-ship when I was fourteen. Then I encountered even more challenges, including the antagonistic and disappointing remarks I heard from my family, professors, and friends. Nonetheless, I yearned for and believed in my success.

Success = idea + faith + endeavor + planning + gratitude

Even my professors created lots of obstacles for me. For instance:

- They didn't allow me to have access to training schools, theater halls, and a rehearsal location.

- They discouraged my actors from attending my rehearsals.
- They created several problems for me in obtaining my official permit.

These were the outcomes. I substituted seven actors and was pushed to change three actors for one role. We had to rehearse in a basement. Our tense rehearsals sometimes took up to ten hours a day. I spent a lot of money and time, and I ended up failing.

Fail, fail well, fail better, always leave a failure room for your A and B plans, have a plan C, and finally make it, thanks be to God.

I searched for a year and invited three nationally recognized art advisors to my group, thanks be to God. Subsequently, I restarted the rehearsals with the new group. More importantly, I believed that our great Creator wishes the best for us.

I experienced numerous challenges again this time, including that I heard many disappointing remarks and was targeted by more and stronger opposition, but I did not fear and never backed off. I heard these remarks many times, so many times: "Barbad, you are crazy. Barbad, your perseverance is admirable." And every time I heard them, I rejoiced more and grew more confident that I was progressing correctly and perfectly, thank God.

I substituted twenty-five actors this time, five actors per each role. Growing exhausted along the way, I decided to back off several times, but I stood up again, put my trust in God Almighty, carried on, and enjoyed the course of events.

I was pushed to select five people who were merely interested in this art, without any performance training under their belts, and I personally trained them, thanks be to God. We rehearsed for some months and sometimes our rehearsals took up to ten or twelve hours a day.

Thank God, I managed to perform in the best theatre hall in Isfahan Province, Iran's Art Cradle, this time when I was sixteen. Again, thank God, I earned the title of Iran's youngest drama director.

If God helps you, none can overcome you.

--The Holy Quran, Al-i-Imran, verse 160

I faced so many challenges over the ten performance nights. For instance, one of my actors told me on the fourth night of performances that he could no longer perform and that he had to take a trip, and he left. I was forced to substitute an actor for him, a very difficult thing to do with a high risk involved.

Then, on the ninth night of our performance, the team member in charge of lighting and sound was stuck in heavy traffic and arrived late. I was forced to do his job until he arrived. There were other challenges as well, all really tough, especially for a sixteen-year-old experiencing drama directorship for the first time.

Thank God, people came from everywhere in the country to watch my play. And I learned big lessons from these performances, which I would never forget:

- Your real age depends on your mental attitude, and not on the number of years you have lived.
- Taking a lesson from postage stamps, they stick to the corner of the envelope until they get to the destination. Ideally, we learn this lesson with one difference: we should enjoy the road too.

On the sixth night of performance, the theatre hall was packed with spectators, such that some had to watch while standing. On the eighth night we had no spectators. This taught me a big lesson. It is true that drama comes with ups and downs, just like life itself. But it is important how you choose to look at it, what are your perspective and worldview. Most of the situations people call a failure are nothing but temporary hardships.

Something really pleasant happened on the last night of performance. The same professors who had created difficulties for me came to watch my play. They applauded and admired my work and the actors very much at the end of the play. They acknowledged that this play, and especially its directorship, was comparable to those performed in the capital city. They asked my actors to perform in their upcoming plays. They also acknowledged their high-performance capabilities, asking them in which institute they had been trained. One of my project advisers answered, "They are Barbad's students and Barbad trained them."

I became so pleased and delighted with this occasion and, thank God, it made me proud. Once my performances were over, I was so pleased and thankful to God for this great honor of directorship at that age and that I managed to train some agreeable actors.

My dear friend, I failed, and I finally made it. I managed to tackle the challenges prior to, during, and after the performances, thank God. It was a delightful feeling that taught me everything ends well. If something is not well, then it is not the end of it. God wanted it, so we give thanks to God.

Dear fellow, you too can experience feelings of pleasure after facing adversities. Whenever you face a difficulty in your life, suppose that you are standing on top of the highest mountain you know and from there look down at your difficulty or challenge and see how tiny it is, if not invisible. With that perspective, you can solve it. Your Lord is the Creator of the universe, so you can do it.

Three years after all these adventures, and at the age of nineteen, I am thankful to God that I could earn my international directorship certificate from UNESCO. O God, thank you.

Dear friend, here are some hints that helped me progress:

   1. You are the master of your own fate; this is a divine

blessing.

2. One of the important pillars of success is daily thanksgiving.

3. Some opportunities manifest themselves in the form of temporary failures at first glance.

4. Silently move forward and be humble.

5. Love yourself very much.

6. Have faith in God's planning for His servants' lives.

7. God has always been from the beginning, and He will also be from now till the end.

Our accomplishments in life are the results of our mental strategy. In my opinion, two of the important bases of such strategy are daily thanksgiving and self-discipline, enabling us to accomplish in the best possible way.

When?

- Whenever you tried and did not stop.
- Whenever you failed and did not back off.
- Whenever you developed a wholehearted belief in your success.

Why?

- Because we are created by God, who is the Creator of the whole universe.
- Because we deserve individual and social accomplishments.

Where?

- It happens wherever it should happen, so be not hasty. Let's put our trust in God the Most Merciful, the Most Benevolent.

Here, I take the opportunity to thank my family, who helped me so much, especially on the nights before the performance of the plays I directed, and to tell them that I love them. Our families go to a lot of trouble and endure so much hardship to raise us as children, and they encounter various challenges. I kiss their hands from where I stand now, and I would like to tell them that we children are so proud of their presence.

My dear friend, I am so grateful that you took a step towards success by reading this book. O dear God, thank you.

Why? When? Where?
Rising above
Challenge and
Adversity

Author's Bio

In the Name of God, who is the Kindest of all Benevolent A door that is opened by God may not be closed by another. **Barbad Raeisi** is a theater actor and director whose works of art have an audience from all across the world. This audience includes people who highly value themselves, their capital, their viewpoints, and their soul and spirit. Barbad is in charge of producing his works and is an expert in cryptocurrency and Blockchain. Barbad gives advice to and guides individuals and companies who are seeking a tomorrow which is more favorable than today. Barbad's great skill in consulting is that he is able to multiply the capital of his clients in a short period of time. In better words, he has multiplied the capital of his clients by 800 to 1300 times in the last year alone. This is mind-blowing!

His clients often say: "Barbad does miracles with our capital!" and "When we follow his guidelines and advice, we are sure to be winners."

His instructor says, "When we are talking about a student being better that his/her instructor, we mean precisely Barbad."

Until the time this text is being written, Barbad is capable of introducing six approaches that will make you richer than you are today, in the shortest time possible, in the field of cryptocurrency and Blockchain.

Barbad has the honor of performing actual miracles with a satisfaction rate of 97% of his clients. He, of course, believes that this is due to the grace and indulgence of God Almighty.

Barbad has ten years of beaming experience in acting and directing. Some of his honors are as follows:

- International Acting Certificate issued from France
- International Acting Certificate issued from Italy
- International Acting Certificate issued from Iran
- International Certificate in Directing issued from UNESCO
- International Certificate in Screenwriting issued from UNESCO

- Being the youngest theater director in Iran

Furthermore, Barbad cherishes a love for Iranian literature, which has greatly contributed to and influenced his life, thank God. He is a co-author of *Covid Acts of Kindness* and GUINNESS WORLD RECORD participant of "Most Authors Signing the Same Book Simultaneously".

The future belongs to the cryptocurrency market, and by making wise and thoughtful investments in the Blockchain platform, you can ensure a peaceful living for yourself and your family and guarantee your capital. It is our great honor for you to have this wonderful experience with Barbad Raeisi, whose clients have been able to make high-percentage profits from this market.

To arrange a consultation session, please contact the provided WhatsApp number or email address. Thank God for his endless mercy.

For many years now, Barbad has been working an average of 60 to 70 hours per week to make sure he is among the very best in his field and his clients can invest in the right places.

Contact Barbad at:

📞 (+98) 9333585389
📷 barbad_raeisi
✉️ barbad.raeisi121@gmail.com

The Reward of

Perseverance

Kris Safarova

The Reward of Perseverance

Kris Safarova

Clients often see a summary of my life spread over three continents, from master classical concert pianist to management consultant to corporate banker to business owner, and they want to know how I built a successful career. It did not start this way and I have found the best lessons come not from my successes but from mining the chokeholds in my life for the patterns that gave me the resiliency to persevere.

When I was young and aspired for more than what society had intended for me, the universe seemed to be giving me many signals to make peace with my life. I went from working as a musician making $2.50 a day to my first job in the West, which involved dragging heavy bags of mail through the streets of Johannesburg, South Africa. There I earned $500 a month with no medical or dental insurance and lived in an apartment with cockroaches. Did you know African cockroaches have wings and fly right at you when you surprise them?

I have been told by many of my mentees and students that the principles distilled from my life experiences have helped them remove the mental blocks in their minds by giving them insights, greater confidence, hope and a sense of community. Therefore, I am going to share some of them with you.

There was an incident which I remember vividly, even though it took place almost four decades ago. I had just turned three years old and was living with my parents in Kuibyshev City— which is now known as Samara—in the southeastern part of European Russia, on the banks of the Volga River.

Both of my parents had to work extremely hard for our family to survive in the chaotic years around the collapse of the Former Soviet Union. One morning our landlord suddenly asked us to move out by the end of the day. It was totally unexpected, and we had no legal recourse. I still recall to this day how I had to walk through the knee-high snow with my parents, who were carrying my newborn twin brothers and our belongings on the sledge, trudging through the night.

It is also true that in the business world, regardless of how much we plan, we must always expect the unexpected. It's good practice to continuously review the worst-case scenarios for both our lives and our careers. And it's important to be mentally and financially ready to deal with adversity.

When my parents faced this challenge as a young couple with three children, they did not have the professional training or the corporate exposure I now have. In addition, my father is Azerbaijani, and we had to deal with persistent discrimination. My parents had to make quick decisions; within minutes of being told to leave, they already knew what to do next.

They knew to only take with them what was most important

that would allow them to restart life as soon as possible with minimal regret. It's easy to assume this is the normal response in a crisis, but experience will teach you that it is common to react emotionally and make the wrong decisions in the heat (or, on a lighter note, the cold) of the moment.

I found that an effective way to avoid making an emotional decision is to visualize your critical path towards your goals and imagine what could go wrong.

I have also learned to understand, accept, and move on with parts of business or life over which I have little control. As an example, I have faced, and continue to face, many forms of discrimination. I just keep moving forward. I will not allow someone else's prejudicial opinion of me to determine my reality.

Going back to the story I was sharing earlier, when I was fighting so hard to walk with my tiny legs through the heavy snow, while the Russian winter was biting my cheeks, I am sure my parents wanted to help me. Yet, they could not help me since they already had twin newborn babies and all our belongings in their care. Putting me on the sledge would have resulted in them leaving behind some of our belongings.

Trade-offs and Embracing Crisis Moments

In business and life in general, we quite often come across situations requiring a trade-off. The toughest of these situations and the decisions we make to prioritize what we truly need can radically alter the trajectory of our life for the better, if we manage them correctly. This is because when you are forced to choose what you really need to survive, you are forced to answer the question of where you are going in life. Without these crisis moments we often get trapped in routines that don't take us to where we want to go in life. We need to embrace problems because they snap us out of our routines by forcing us to reconsider what we truly value, by making us rethink our key goals for our life.

I often hear from my mentees and colleagues that they just want to know the best practices I follow or those another business leader follows. I counsel them to learn the best practices but also understand the goal the leader was trying to achieve and their unique circumstances. If you are pursuing a different goal with different circumstances, it's important to adjust the best practice so that it works for you. For example, when I started out building my businesses, I knew all successful leaders delegated as much as they could. At first, I did not have the money to hire people. This was my unique circumstance, so I tried to prioritize and simplify things until I could hire people.

To make this adjustment, you need to tap your vast reservoir of past experiences to know how you responded in the past, what you have learned and how you could respond to the problem today. In other words, just as I use my experiences to shape my decisions, so should you.

Looking back at the story I was sharing, there was no option but to accept the fact that my parents' hands were full and there was no space for me on the sledge. I was lucky to have the strength to keep lifting my legs high, in my winter coat. In hindsight I am happy that I could help my parents during one of the toughest situations they ever had to endure, by trying to put on a brave face and not making their life harder than it already was.

The Balancing Act of Risks and Rewards

Making any decision is a continuous balancing act between knowing the rewards and the calculated risks you are taking, and how those will unfold once the decision is made. I also gently remind clients that the risks are dependent not only on the confidence level one has but on your level of resourcefulness. The plan worked because I, as a three-year-old, was resourceful to not give up and kept lifting my legs high enough to make every step required to finish that journey.

Clients often focus on the resources at their disposal when confronted with a challenge, and they frequently view their ability to respond as being directly proportional to the sum of their resources. In other words, they think the greater the resources they have before starting, the greater their odds of success. I have seen many talented clients adopt a resources-based view of life and give up on potentially lucrative paths because they wanted the comfort of having the right resources in place to back them up before proceeding.

Resourcefulness, in contrast, is a belief in yourself that you will eventually assemble the resources you need or discover a better way to move forward with fewer resources. You proceed before waiting for the resources to show up. You trust yourself to learn, adjust and build allies as you proceed. Your *raison d'etre*, your "why" as such, is so strong and compelling that you know you will find a way to overcome the challenge.

In my own life, I have had to be resourceful because I had practically no resources starting out. I could not get a visa interview for most countries, and I barely spoke English. When I did get a visa to South Africa, I only had about US$1,000 in savings. I struggled to get any job for a long time and did not have an education that was accredited in the West. I had to find ways to move forward without losing myself in the process. I often took a step or two back to ultimately get me where I wanted to go. I was constantly assessing the returns and the risks. Often, after incurring significant costs on a plan, I would realize it was not working. I would then persist and pivot to find a new plan to reach my goals.

In case you were wondering what happened after our landlord asked us to leave by the end of the day in the middle of Russian winter conditions, for a few days we were without a home. Yet, we had each other as a family, and we asked friends if we could spend a few nights at a time in their homes. Sadly, this would not be the last time in my life I would be without a home, penniless, or fearing for my life.

Strength Found in Adversity

Today, I can say I have been enriched by those life experiences. When I talk to clients from around the world, I know the tough choices they had to make, and some still must make, between food, getting an education or building a business. There was a point in my life when I could not afford the smallest KFC mash and gravy portion for lunch and often skipped lunch. I know the indignity of being rejected after hundreds of job applications. I know what it's like to go back to university when you are twenty-five while working full time, and in my case, barely understanding the language of instruction. I know the humiliation of being thirty with only $76 in my bank account and trying to find a way to pay for my education. I share this with you because I am a product of adversity. I want you to be resilient, and it helps when you know others have been where you are and made it while keeping true to themselves.

Those experiences have made me stronger. I build products, services, and businesses for people who want the dignity of making a difference on their terms. That's the reward of perseverance. When you come out on the other side you have a new appreciation for what people truly face in the world.

Now that you overcame your adversity, you have hope and a roadmap to help others. I feel it's my duty to share that roadmap and guide others.

I have seen my parents not taking "no" for an answer and not giving up, even in the harshest conditions, as they knew they had to ensure survival for their family. They knew that not everything in life comes served on a silver platter, and they also knew where to compromise and where to be flexible in the pursuit of happiness.

Over time, I have realized that "no" often does not mean "never"- if you do not give up. Sometimes it means "maybe" or "not now." If you keep on working, you may very well get what you want.

COVID-19 and all that it unleashed created a new wave of challenges. Specifically, businesses are forced to become comfortable with remotely managing employees and functions they never would have considered managing off premises. Professions and skills that were rarely at risk for outsourcing and offshoring, are now at risk.

We don't know how this will eventually play out. Yet, employees need to learn new skills to build rapport, project confidence, have an executive presence and gravitas, while operating remotely. Networking and mentoring are changing, and the way we build those informal alliances over lunch or coffee, that are crucial to getting us plum assignments and promotions, is changing too.

All these challenges will create opportunities to learn and adjust. They should be embraced. Treat each one as a chance to build your library of critical life lessons. In a world where more and more work can be outsourced and offshored, you need to build your brand as someone who truly adds the most value in the world for the work you do. That is the ultimate persistence muscle you will need to build.

When I look back on the stories I shared with you, I am truly grateful for the life I had. There is very little that can intimidate me after having lived in the Former Soviet Union and needing to stand in line for hours to *maybe* bring home one loaf of bread or one stick of margarine. It's hard for me to get upset about bad customer service in an airconditioned mall after getting locked in the office of a gasoline station after an interview that went horribly wrong. Of course, this was all much better than the time someone kidnapped me, and I waited to escape when all his armed security fell asleep, or the time a man chased me down the streets in broad daylight while shouting profanity because I would not get into his car, and I had to run to my friend's apartment to hide.

If you are reading this and you are going through similar experiences as I did, my message to you is not to stop. If you pick yourself up each day, ask questions and keep trying, you are giving yourself a great chance to make it. I cannot sugarcoat this. You will hate the tough moments, but you will likely one day realize they were a blessing that allowed you to break through. They will become your emotional shield.

A strong *why* will fuel your persistence. This is the one true source of persistence. You need to know why you were put on this planet and why you must succeed. When things become truly difficult and seemingly hopeless, a strong why will give you the strength you need to not give up.

Persistence by itself, however, is insufficient. Persistence pays off if you know the goal you want to achieve. You learn from your own experiences while adapting the best practices of those who have done what you want to do, and you fully commit to acting on your intentions.

I wake up each day and I still work the same long hours. However, now it's my choice, and I get to do what I want to do by helping people around the world and leading successful businesses. I do not want anyone anywhere in the world to settle for a life of misery and suffering. I want you to aspire to more than what society had intended for you.

That's my *why*. You need to find yours.

The Reward of
Perseverance

Author's Bio

Kris Safarova is a bestselling author and
entrepreneur with extensive experience in online businesses,
publishing, and consulting.

She manages a portfolio of companies, which includes the
world's largest strategy and consulting business-building
training platforms, StrategyTraining.com and Firmsconsulting.
com, and she studied under Roger Love to become a reputed
and certified speaking coach.

Kris also manages two iTunes career podcasts ranked in
the top ten in many countries -"Strategy Skills" and "Case

Interviews & Management Consulting."

She holds an MBA from Ivey Business School in Canada, graduating on the dean's list with highest distinction. Prior to her MBA, Kris worked in management consulting, and following her MBA, she worked as a corporate banker and managed a portfolio worth more than US$1 billion.

Before entering the consulting industry, Kris was a master classical concert pianist and official music representative of the Russian Federation, who toured Europe. Kris Safarova is a professional with a decades-long track record of rapid promotions in the corporate world and building successful businesses.

If you would like to see the underlying model for Kris's businesses and how you can replicate the model, download it at:

🌐 www.firmsconsulting.com/model

Published by North Star Success Inc.

🌐 www.northstarsuccess.com

✉ support@northstarsuccess.com

📞 +1 647 479 0790

NORTHSTAR SUCCESS

Build Your Brand.
Grow Your Business.
Make More Impact.

We provide the ROAD MAP and SOLUTIONS for you to become the trusted authority in your field so you can make the impact you have always wanted to make.

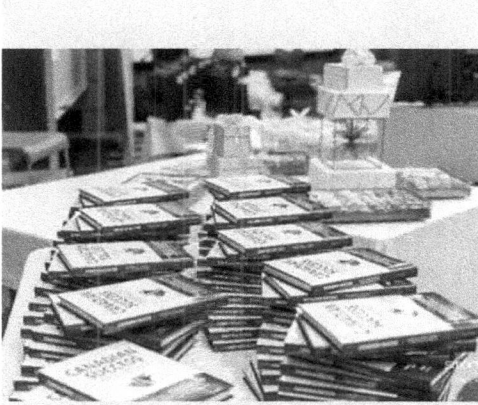

Build Your Brand

Some people write books to build their brand and grow their business. Rise above your competition, differentiate yourself from the crowd, and create trust like never before.

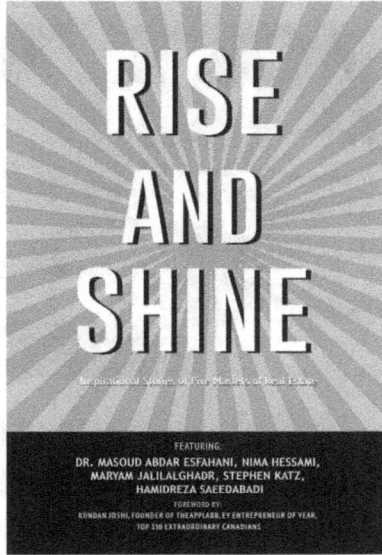

Leave a Legacy

Books are amazing assets to tell your story (or your company's story) and leave a legacy. Let the future generations know about your life/business journey.

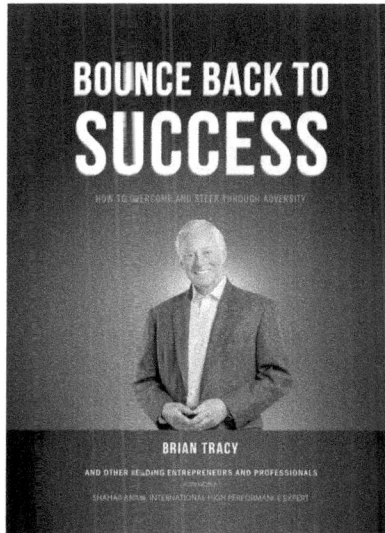

BOUNCE BACK TO SUCCESS

HOW TO OVERCOME AND STEER THROUGH ADVERSITY

BRIAN TRACY

AND OTHER LEADING ENTREPRENEURS AND PROFESSIONALS

SHAHAB ANARI, INTERNATIONAL HIGH PERFORMANCE EXPERT

One Chapter or a Whole Book

It could be a chapter in our next multi-author book. It could also be your very own whole book.